ATLANTIS
THE FIND OF A LIFETIME

CHRISTOS A. DJONIS

PAGE PUBLISHING, INC.
Conneaut Lake, PA

First originally published by Page Publishing 2021

ISBN 978-1-6624-4259-9 (pbk)
ISBN 978-1-6624-4127-1 (hc)
ISBN 978-1-6624-4126-4 (digital)

Printed in the United States of America

If you have only one piece of circumstantial evidence, carrying that evidence to a specific conclusion is prone to significant error. However, when you have numerous pieces of circumstantial evidence all pointing in the same direction, carrying them, collectively, to a specific conclusion is usually quite reliable.
Conclusions Drawn from Circumstantial Evidence

CONTENTS

INTRODUCTION

Nearly 2,400 years ago, the ancient philosopher Plato wrote the story of Atlantis, a compelling tale of an 11,000-year-old island civilization that since captivated the imagination of poets, authors, and many scholars' minds who unsuccessfully, over the centuries, kept on searching for the elusive island.

Numerous speculations and proposed locations over the years place Atlantis in the middle of the Atlantic around the Azores Islands, in Spain, off the coast of Cyprus, in Malta, and in other more exotic locations like Indonesia, Antarctica, in the "Bermuda Triangle" off the coast of the United States, and a dozen other places around the world. While, of course, some of these claims over the years were noted more than others, the fact is, never has there been a real discovery where all the physical characteristics of a proposed location matched Plato's description or given chronology. Not even the popular Santorini hypothesis could adequately meet the given criteria. Plato's specified chronology was entirely discarded by those who proposed the original theory while the primary island of Atlantis, a massive island that was supposed to be 9 kilometers away from the circular island-within-an-island setting, is entirely missing from the Santorini backdrop of 1,600 BC. This, along with several other inconsistencies, was the reason why skeptics in the past dismissed the Santorini hypothesis and continued to adhere to their claim that Plato's story was just a cautionary tale.

Were the Atlanteans a truly prehistoric civilization as Plato claimed, or was that a myth? Was the story of Atlantis entirely a product of Plato's imagination, or is it possible he created a fable around a real setting and a prehistoric civilization known to ancient Greeks, which, in order to successfully communicate some of his philosophical ideas (divine vs. human, ideal societies vs. corrupt), he applied familiar matter and details from his own era, just as Homer did with Troy a few hundred years earlier. In Troy's case, after ditching all the details regarding beauty queens, demigods, and Trojan horses and scaled back the armies to more rational levels, it was ultimately acknowledged that the setting, as well as the bulk of this story, was real. Essentially, Homer's entirely fictional story, which he filled with principles and elements from his own period, apparently revolved around an actual setting and a real incident that took place nearly six centuries before his time.

So if Plato did with Atlantis what Homer did with Iliad, then just as in Troy's case, the "true part" of this story should not rest in the story details but in the detection and authentication of Plato's "lost island." Locating a perfectly matching site and, along with it, signs of a prehistoric civilization in the immediate area should be the first step in solving this mystery.

After years of extensive research, in conjunction with new archaeological evidence, and with the aid of satellite technology, we now have a real discovery of a prehistoric partially submerged setting where all the physical characteristics, along with Plato's given chronology, perfectly match. DNA and archaeological evidence of an advanced Neolithic civilization occupying the prehistoric submerged island, at around 9,600 BC, further confirms a perfect case scenario.

Embark on a chronicled 10,000-year epic journey that reveals Atlantis's submerged island, and find out how Plato's 2,000-year-old legend transforms into real history.

ATLANTIS REVEALED

*Was the Great Flood a Real Event?—Was North America Colonized by
a Mediterranean Culture 11,000 Years Ago?—The Kennewick Man.
Did a Bronze Age Visitor Help the Mayan Establish Their Civilization?
The Metcalf Stone. Who Were the Minoans?—Atlantis Revealed.
The Great Sphinx: Older Than the Pyramids? Who Erected
Stonehenge? The Meaning Behind the Stone Circles of Europe.
Who Were the Clovis People? The Phaistos Disc.*

While the twentieth century brought to us some of the most incredible scientific breakthroughs humanity ever witnessed, we must not discount the fantastic achievements and technological wonders left behind by past human civilizations. Aside from the several megalithic monuments antiquity left behind, there are also many smaller marvels of ancient ingenuity that confront our awareness and demonstrate our ancestors' exceptional technological abilities.

Excavations on the Greek island of Santorini (Thera) revealed that the 3,600-year-old Bronze Age city of Akrotiri featured advanced multilevel housing structures with indoor plumbing, complete with sewer and water supply lines for both hot and cold water.

This discovery is incredible because up until recently, we were under the impression that it was the Romans who were first able to utilize such technology, nearly 1,500 years later.

The Bronze Age city of Akrotiri on the island of Santorini (Thera) Greece

What about the Antikythera Mechanism (an extremely complex device designed to calculate astronomical positions at any given moment in time)? It was found at the bottom of the Aegean Sea near the Greek island of Antikythera, hence its name. Made of several bronze wheels and other mechanical components more than 2,000 years ago, this device is so incredible that, at first glance, it resembles a twentieth-century piece of equipment. Indeed, when it was first discovered, it was mistaken as such. An x-ray of the mechanism revealed that instruments of this complexity were not known to exist at least until the seventeenth century.

Who designed and constructed this remarkable device or how this technology was lost afterward is not entirely clear. Labeled by scientists as the first mechanical computer in history, this incredible feat of engineering required that its maker had advanced knowledge of astronomy, as well as a diverse knowledge in mechanics and machine making.

*The Antikythera Mechanism displayed at the National
Archaeological Museum of Athens, Greece*

After 75 years deciphering the mechanism, researchers concluded that the ancient device was used as a type of timepiece, based on a geocentric view of the universe. However, instead of hours and minutes, it displayed celestial time and had different hands for the Sun, the Moon, and the five planets visible to the naked eye (Mercury, Venus, Mars, Jupiter, and Saturn). A rotating ball showed the Moon, while dials' phase on the back acted as a calendar and showed lunar and solar eclipses. Captions explained which stars rose and set on any particular date. The most incredible part about this mechanism is that the mechanical gears' precision, which accurately showed all planetary motions, was based on mathematics.

How accurate was the ancient computer, one may ask? It is believed that the planetary motion was accurate to one degree in 500 years.

Professor Michael Edmunds of Cardiff University, who led the most recent study of the mechanism, said,

> This device is just extraordinary, the only thing of its kind. The design is beautiful, the astronomy is exactly right. The way the mechanics are designed just makes your jaw drop. Whoever has done this has done it extremely carefully… in terms of historic and scarcity value, I have to regard this mechanism as being more valuable than the Mona Lisa.[1]

Another one of the many yet unexplained artifacts that continuously raises eyebrows and stirs many debates among the scientific community is the famous Baghdad Battery. This primitive version of a modern battery made from clay vessels, copper tubes, and the right alkaline fluid could produce electricity nearly 2,000 years ago.

In 1938, while working in Khujut Rabu, just outside Baghdad in modern-day Iraq, German archaeologist Wilhelm Konig unearthed the ancient artifact, a 5-inch-long clay jar containing a copper cylinder that encased an iron rod. The container showed signs of corrosion, and early tests revealed that an acidic agent, such as vinegar or wine, had to be stored in it. Many replicas made over time, including by university students, proved that the Baghdad batteries could actually conduct an electric current.

What was the purpose of the electricity produced by these batteries, and where did this knowledge come from, no one really knows. Until their discovery, we were under the impression that battery technology was an eighteenth-century invention.

One more ancient invention by the Greeks that led to the "discovery" of the modern steam engine was the aeolipile, also known as Hero's engine. The aeolipile, described in detail by Hero of Alexandria in the first century BC, is considered the first-ever recorded steam engine or reaction steam turbine device. The name—derived from the Greek word Αἴολος (Aeolus) and the Latin word *pila*—translates to "the ball of Aeolus," Aeolus being the Greek god of the air and wind. The mechanism was a simple, radial steam turbine that spins when the central water container is heated. The torque is produced by steam jets exiting the turbine, much like a rocket engine.

A modern replica of the Hero's engine

With every new find, without a doubt, our ancestors continue to demonstrate that several millennia ago, they were extremely knowledgeable and more technologically advanced than we have been giving them credit for. How, though, did they come across their incredible knowledge? How could they possess skills that, until recently, we thought were acquired during the Industrial Revolution? Were these really brand-new skills, or is it possible that we evolved much earlier in time and slowly developed many of our technological capabilities over the millennia, long before our recorded history? If so, if truly our ancestors had advanced thousands of years earlier than anthropologists previously thought, then what happened to all past human development?

The story of a "Great Flood" sent by God (or gods according to much earlier testimony) to destroy humanity for its "sins" is a widespread account shared by many religions and cultures around the world, and it dates back to our earliest recorded history. From India to ancient Greece, Mesopotamia, and even among North American Indian tribes, there is no shortage of such tales that often enough sound very much alike. Some of these stories sound so similar that one could wonder whether all cultures around the world had experienced such an event. Or is it possible they influenced each other by storytelling over the millennia?

Can it be that all flood accounts so zealously repeated around the world are a collection of myths or isolated incidents? Or was the Great Flood a single worldwide cataclysm that affected all humanity at one point during our prehistory? While small isolated disasters can stress and frighten affected populations equally, their overall effect is short-lived, and they often fade from memory within decades, if not years. In the case of the Great Flood, however, we have a story that seems to have no boundaries and one that every ancient culture insists on its worldwide nature. How big and how destructive, though, was such a disaster that managed to sear itself into our ancestors' collective memory for thousands of years? Judging by the shared testimony, this must not only have been an event that affected everyone simultaneously, but for it to have become a permanent fixture in the human psyche, it must have been an experience that persisted not only for days or months but for several generations.

Today, although science accepts that regional floods have indeed adversely affected many ancient populations over the millennia, it still denies that there was ever a single deluge that affected every civilization on the planet at once. Meanwhile, as the type, chronology, and magnitude of such an event are still highly debated, several scientific theories of the Great Flood are currently in circulation, and more of them continue to surface from time to time.

In recent years, and according to a published study in 1997 by William Ryan and Walter Pitman, the Great Flood story was linked to the "sudden flood" of the Black Sea. According to their hypothesis, at around 5,600 BC, the melting of the glaciers—along with several other significant hydrologic factors that included the flow of rivers and heavy rainfall—caused the Mediterranean Sea level to rise so rapidly that it ultimately and violently flooded the Black Sea, making it into the body of water we know today.

Ryan and Pitman speculated that the Mediterranean's flooding occurred via a massive waterfall, nearly two hundred times larger than that of Niagara Falls, which daily dumped 10 cubic miles of seawater into the Black Sea for 300 days. By the time it was over, 60,000 square miles around the Black Sea had been submerged. This was the best evidence we had for nearly a decade to explain the Great Flood story. Although more of a regional flood, undoubt-edly, such an event could have utterly destroyed any established civilization around the Black Sea during this period and rightfully so could have been labeled as a Great Flood by those who experi-enced it.

Unfortunately for the Ryan and Pitman team, though, another study was conducted since reported differently. Although the later research agreed to the premise of the Black Sea being flooded, it contradicted the severity of the flood as well as the chronological time of the event. In 2005, a research project under UNESCO's sponsorship was conducted by the International Union of Geological Sciences and a Ukrainian and Russian scientific team that included Valentina Yanko-Hoback. They published in 2009 that the Black Sea flood was more of a gradual event and less catastrophic to human life than pre-viously thought. Most importantly, it was determined that the inci-dent took place earlier chronologically and much closer to 8,000 BC. In essence, this study confirmed that the Black Sea's flooding did not have the horrible devastation associated with the loss of human life, and unlike previous estimates, this event took place during our prehistory.

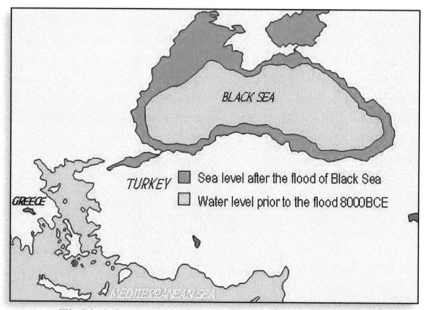

The Black Sea water level before and after the flood of 8,000 BC

If not the Black Sea's flooding, though, what other regional—or better yet—worldwide catastrophe qualifies to be called the Great Flood? Without a doubt, it was the rise of the oceans at the end of the last Ice Age, more particularly the oceans' abrupt rise around 8,000 BC, which led to the Mediterranean's flooding first and, ultimately, to the flooding of the Black Sea. That was the single, long-lasting event that drastically reshaped our planet's coastlines and the one that simultaneously affected every coastal civilization around the world at the time. If past periodic Ice Ages and floods, over millions of years, did not manage to add salinity into the fresh water of the Black Sea (a freshwater lake until that point), then undoubtedly the last global flood around 8,000 BC must have been the "greatest" flood of all time.

Although adverse weather conditions, tsunamis, or hurricane-related floods can cause severe destruction several miles inland, the effects of such disasters are always temporary. The oceans' significant rise, however—a worldwide catastrophe that erased millions of square miles of dryland around the planet—must have been the doomsday event every culture to this day inadvertently is talking about. Even when at first look the gradual rise of the oceans does not seem to meet the criteria as the event behind the legend of the Great Flood, an incident responsible for the sea level to rise globally by more than 400 feet, surely had many random episodes when the flooding was unpredictable. When considering that humans, by nature, tend to settle in lower elevations and near water, it leaves no doubt that all prehistoric civilizations were devastated by this event. This must have been a constant relocation and adjustment period as people continuously kept on looking for higher ground to rebuild and new valleys to grow crops to support those settlements.

To challenge this theory, at least until recently, anthropologists insisted that 10,000 years ago, humans were way too primitive to have been aware of such an event. So in essence, as there were no known civilizations around at the time that could have been affected by this natural catastrophe, the Great Flood story was thought to be a myth or a disaster that has taken place later in time, during our recorded history. Of course, as there are no clues of global cataclysms during our recorded history, this once more led to their eventual conclusion that the Great Flood was either a myth or a much smaller regional incident like the flooding of the Black Sea.

For many years, this was the general "logic" that dominated many academic minds and the greatest challenge to the Ice Age flood theory when this hypothesis was brought up.

Incidentally, all this changed in 1994 with the archaeological discovery of Gobekli Tepe, a 12,000-year-old megasite in southeastern Turkey, and a few years later, in 2002, with the discovery of a 10,000-year-old city found submerged under 130 feet of water off the coast of West

India in the Gulf of Cambay. In this case, several generations of fishermen insisted on stories of an underwater city in that area. Still, their claims went unnoticed until the site was accidentally discovered during pollution survey tests conducted by India's National Institute of Ocean Technology. With the use of side-scan sonar, which sends a beam of sound waves to the bottom of the ocean, scientists found massive geometric structures at a depth of about 120 feet. Dredging debris and more than two thousand artifacts recovered from the site, including construction material, pottery, sections of walls, beads, sculptures, and human bones, had been carbon-dated and found to be approximately 10,000 years old.

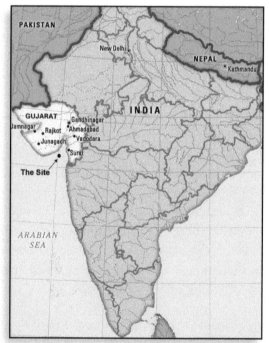

The location of the underwater city (Gulf of Cambay)

Archaeologists later determined that the submerged city, which stretched along the banks of an ancient riverbed, bore striking similarities to Indus Valley Civilization sites in the mainland. One of its structures, an Olympic-size swimming pool, had a series of sunken steps that looked like the Great Bath of Mohenjo Daro. Another rectangular platform was 200 meters long and 45 meters wide—as big as the acropolis found in Harappa.

Scientists now estimate that this 10-square-mile city was sunken after the last Ice Age when melting ice caused the oceans worldwide to rise significantly. This was an incredible find. Not only does this discovery help rewrite some of the early pages of our history, but most importantly, it confirms ancient testimony regarding earlier lost civilizations.

Of course, in addition to these two recent remarkable discoveries, let us not ignore the fact that several more archaeological sites dating between the ninth and tenth millennium BC prove that humankind had advanced much earlier than previously thought. The ancient city of Jericho, which some of its structures date back to the tenth millennium BC; the Hallan Cemi settlement in Turkey, dating at 9,500 BC; and the Jerf el Ahmar in Syria, which dates at around 9,600 BC not only demonstrate that humans had organized much earlier, but evidence from these sites show that these settlements were ahead of their time. At Jerf el Ahmar, for example, the archaeological team discovered more than forty well-preserved houses, an unbelievable number from this period, all revealing an evolution from circular to rectangular living structures. Archaeologists also discovered small terra-cotta plaquettes bearing mnemonic symbols etched 5,000 years before the appearance of writing and grains, such as wheat, indicating the first traces of cultivation. Indeed, researchers concluded that Jerf el Ahmar was involved in large-scale cereal processing long before cereal domestication. Barley cultivation and systematic food production from wild cereals at this settlement started at around 9,000 BC, nearly a thousand years earlier than previously thought.

Without a doubt, this discovery not only proves that humans had advanced much earlier, but it demonstrates that these people would have been fully aware of any cataclysmic event, like the rise of the oceans and the flooding of the Mediterranean, at around 8,000 BC.

Considering all the latest findings, is it possible today to assume that a worldwide flood, roughly 10,000 years ago, may have been the one our ancestors labeled as the Great Flood? Certainly, we can. The submerged city off the west coast of India, along with the ancient cities named above, not only confirm that 10,000 years ago, humans were more advanced and thus aware of this particular natural catastrophe, but it further proves that the rising waters, particularly between 8,000 BC and 7,500 BC, devastated many prehistoric civilizations and destroyed most evidence of their existence.

In a study published in *Current Anthropology* on December 2010, titled "New Light on Human Prehistory in the Arabo-Persian Gulf Oasis," Jeffrey Rose, an archaeologist and researcher with the United Kingdom's University of Birmingham, pointed out that sixty highly advanced settlements arose out of nowhere around the shores of the Persian Gulf about 7,500 years ago. These settlements featured well-built stone houses, long-distance trade networks, elaborate pottery, and signs of domesticated animals. With no known precursor populations in the archaeological record to explain these advanced settlements' existence, Rose ultimately concluded the dwellers of these new settlements were those of displaced populations who managed to escape the gulf inundation around 8,000 BC.

As more and more evidence points toward such a conclusion, is it so difficult to imagine that such a worldwide cataclysm could have been what erased our early history? If not, how else can we justify the rise of several advanced civilizations around the planet, which seems to mysteriously appear out of thin air since the dawn of our recorded history? Overnight, these people turned out to be masters of architecture and astronomy and somehow possessed incredible technological skills that neither historians nor anthropologists can quite explain. Is it possible that due to the lack of tangible evidence, early scholars failed to make the connection and to recognize that many of these cultures had advanced thousands of years earlier and before the Great Flood? Is it so difficult to accept that the incredible megalithic structures and technological achievements of our early recorded history were essentially part of an earlier "renaissance" era that began once the rise of the oceans ended?

Finally, with all clues pointing that more sunken cities around the planet may be awaiting our discovery (like Pavlopetri, a 5,000-year-old city found submerged in southern Greece, or Atlit Yam, an 11,000-year-old Neolithic city off the coast of Israel), can we safely assume that the rising seas may have been the cataclysm that destroyed yet another legendary civilization, like that of Atlantis?

After all, let us not overlook the fact that several more so-called "mythical places" from antiquity turned out to be true. Troy, for instance, which for centuries was thought to be a creation of Homer's imagination, was ultimately found in western Turkey and in the exact geographic location where Homer had placed it in his story. In the case of Troy, as many established archaeologists refused to search for such a "mythological" place, the burden was taken by Heinrich Schliemann, an amateur archaeologist who ultimately discovered the legendary city by following location tips contained in Homer's epic book, *Iliad*. Could it be then that the rest of Homer's story is real? One thing is sure: After a thorough analysis of the site, which took several decades, archaeologists conceded that the Greeks had burned Troy to the ground, just as Homer asserted in his account.

The infamous cities of Sodom and Gomorrah (otherwise known as Bab-edh-Dhra and Numeira), which, according to the Bible, suffered God's ultimate wrath, were also ultimately discovered and are now sites of continuous study. Incredibly enough, and just as the Bible claims, we have also concluded that both cities were destroyed as if by brimstone and fire. Is this just another strange coincidence? While elevated traces of radiation among the ruins raise legitimate questions about what exactly was "brimstone and fire," one fact remains: The once-imaginary cities were real, and the primitive description of their demise, no matter how fantastic it sounded once, turned out to be correct.

Another such "mythical" city mentioned in the Koran, known to the west as the "Atlantis of the Sands," also known as Ubar, or Iram of the Pillars, was also found in the desert somewhere in the Arabian Peninsula. The ruins of the ancient city, in this case, were found in 1991, when a team of researchers used NASA's *Challenger* radar system to discover hints of the ancient city beneath the sands of Dhofar's northern desert. Later on, expeditions uncovered ruins dating back to 1,000 BC, with fortress walls found to have been built over a massive limestone cave. As the cave collapsed, the small city was engulfed by the desert sands. It is worth noting that even to this day, researchers and archaeologists alike are still puzzled how a city like Ubar could survive—let alone thrive—in a sandy wasteland. This, of course, was the very reason why mainstream academia thought that Ubar must be just another myth.

What about Atlantis, though? Is it possible that Plato's story, first mentioned to Solon by Egyptian priests and then written by Plato 2,400 years ago, was real?

According to the Egyptians, not only was Atlantis a real place, but around 9,600 BC, the Atlanteans were the dominating power in the Mediterranean as they ruled over several parts of southern Europe, North Africa, and the Middle East. Of course, they were not the superadvanced civilization many people during the twentieth century made them out to be but, at best, a civilization equally advanced as that of Plato's at the time. Without the technology we possess today, Plato explained that they were extremely innovative and capable navigators, who frequently traveled into the Atlantic Ocean to explore.

Today, many theories place Atlantis in locations such as off the coast of southeastern Cyprus, outside the Strait of Gibraltar in the middle of the Atlantic, somewhere in the Bermuda Triangle off the coast of the United States, or even in more exotic locations such as Antarctica or the Pacific Ocean. Of course, more mainstream studies point to the tiny island of Santorini; the island of Crete, Malta, and Spain; and other archaeological sites around the Mediterranean. Overall, there are countless theories on Atlantis's location while more seem to surface every year.

Despite the scientific and nonscientific speculations though, since all so-called discoveries thus far either missing elements from Plato's physical description or simply fail to meet Plato's given chronology, most scholars and critics have concluded that Plato's tale of Atlantis must be either a myth, or Plato must have crafted a story while using a mix of real elements from later times. As for the legendary island, since a perfectly matching site eluded us so far, modern historians also tend to think it is not real.

Is it possible then that the story of Atlantis was a figment of Plato's imagination? Anything is possible although if the story is not real, how can we otherwise explain the several pieces of tangible evidence that seem to corroborate this story? And what about Plato's own assurances? Fifteen times in *Timaeus* and seven times in *Critias*, Plato either directly or indirectly insisted that his story was real. Why would he do that? In *Timaeus* alone, Plato stated that the story Solon heard from an Egyptian priest was true, not a mere legend, but a fact. While obviously Plato's insistence does not necessarily make a story real, we must still ask why he put so much emphasis on that unless he truly wanted his audience to believe him and not dismiss the story as a mere myth.

Conclusively, the best evidence to prove Atlantis's existence is to locate the legendary island itself. Such a discovery would not only validate Plato's claim but logically would help end the ongoing debate among skeptics and believers. If Atlantis's island is real, however, why have all past efforts to find it failed? Even if the task of locating a sunken island is not exactly an easy one, when considering our technological abilities, shouldn't we have been able to find it by now?

Actually, there are a couple of explanations why this discovery has eluded us so far. First, a significant problem in solving this mystery was unquestionably the scientific community's pessimistic position on the subject and their refusal to accept that a 12,000-year-old civilization could have ever been possible. Over the years, several discoveries and recent finds that demonstrated that humans had advanced much earlier than previously thought had little or no effect in persuading mainstream academia to pursue the subject. Consequently, since most researchers and archaeologists kept a safe distance from a "radioactive" subject like that of Atlantis, Plato's story and its discovery were ultimately placed in fringe authors and amateur archaeologists' hands. So during the twentieth century, with so many variations of Plato's story produced by fiction authors, for many believers, Atlantis erroneously turned out to be this ultramodern civilization that was technologically more advanced than our own.

Another problem that often complicated the search was our failure to read and accurately translate Plato's story from ancient Greek to English without allowing personal understandings to interfere. Simple errors and flawed interpretations made by early translators led many in the past to look for Atlantis in all the wrong places. This failure to correctly translate Plato's story and our inability to apply more common sense when reading Plato's text made our search even more difficult than it had to be. Simply put, if (according to Plato) Atlantis was the dominating power within the Mediterranean, shouldn't this revelation alone lead to the logical assumption that as an island, it should have been somewhere within the Mediterranean as well? On the other hand, the mere mention of another grand island/continent across the Atlantic, outside the Pillars of Hercules (one Plato described as "larger than Libya and Asia put together"), often enough stirs people's imaginations as well as their natural tendencies to go after bigger and more exciting things. This internal drive often causes many people to overlook the smaller tangible clues and to go after that "grand island" on the other side of the Atlantic since "bigger is always better." This is akin to the fable of *The Dog and Its Reflection*, where a dog carries a small bone, looks down as it crosses a stream, and sees its reflection in the water. Thinking that his reflection was another dog carrying a bigger bone, the dog opens its mouth to grab the larger bone from the "other" dog and, in doing so, drops and loses the bone it was carrying.

Indeed, when the document is closely examined and accurately translated, we see that Plato did not say Atlantis was located on the other side of the Atlantic, but rather, he pointed to the fact that the Atlanteans were capable of crossing outside the Pillars of Hercules (Strait of Gibraltar) into the Atlantic, and by following the islands that "encompassed that veritable ocean," they were able to reach another "grand island," or better yet, a continent on the other side of the Atlantic, one larger than Libya and Asia combined.

Before attempting to make sense out of a translated document, those not familiar with ancient Greek must know that the syntactic structure of the language that Plato used has a very different structure than the English language we often use to translate it. For instance, the simple English phrase "the queen began to talk" translates to Greek as "began to talk, the queen." What often seems strange to those who first try to learn Greek is the inversion of the possessive adjective with respect to the noun. Similarly, text inversions like these may also exist in the sequence of entire sentences. For example, in an independent clause, an item that is stressed, that is, uttered with emphasis or contrastive, in ancient Greek generally goes at the beginning of the clause, rarely at the end. The middle position is occupied by an item receiving no particular emphasis. In a series of clauses, though, a prominent item goes at the beginning of its clause if it relates to the previous context and at the end if it relates to the following one.

In other words, the real emphasis on the following translated text from *Timaeus* (24e) should be placed on the first sentence of the first paragraph, as well as on the first and last sentence of the second one (*highlighted in bold italic*). Each paragraph's remaining text provides supportive information and should be read last (even if to an English reader that seems to defy logic).

> *For it is related in our records how once upon a time your State stayed the course of a mighty host,* which, starting from a distant point in the Atlantic Ocean, was insolently advancing to attack the whole of Europe, and Asia to boot.

> *(For) the Ocean that was at that time navigable;* for in front of the mouth which you Greeks call, as you say "the Pillars of Hercules" [Strait of Gibraltar] there lay an island which was larger than Libya and Asia together; *and it was possible for travelers of that time to cross from it to the other islands and from the islands to the whole of the continent over against them which encompasses the veritable ocean.*[2]

In this case, and contrary to what many automatically assume, when reading the ancient text in the proper syntactic structure, Plato does not point to Atlantis's direction across the ocean. As explained earlier, the phrase *"your state stayed the course of a mighty host"* is where the emphasis first should be placed at the beginning of the clause. While in this sentence Plato reveals the very close proximity of Atlantis to Greece, in the rest of the sentence, he poetically describes Atlantis's might and its capacity that stretched around the world to a "distant point," and another continent, across the ocean. Once he illustrates their incredible capabilities to the audience, he then describes their audacious and warlike nature and their plans to "advance against the whole of Europe and Asia."

The same rule applies when analyzing the remaining text. In this case, the revelation of a continent across the ocean is not where the emphasis should be placed. As explained earlier, in a series of sentences in a clause, prominent items usually are either placed at the beginning or the end of their clause. The middle part of a clause is occupied by items that should receive less emphasis. According to this rule, the revelation that *"the Atlantic Ocean was naviga-*

ble" at the time, at the beginning of the second paragraph, and the explanation how the Atlanteans were able to reach another continent across the ocean via island hopping (at the end of the clause), is where the emphasis should be placed and not on the continent itself mentioned in the middle of the clause (the part that many automatically are drawn to). In this case, the middle sentence provides supportive information and simply reveals how enormous is the continent across the ocean.

Not knowing where the emphasis on a clause should be placed can cause a great deal of confusion as often, and depending on where the emphasis goes, two separate meanings can emerge out of a single paragraph. Sometimes, even a single comma can cause a short sentence to have two different meanings when it comes to ancient Greek. Such an example is a famous quote from the Oracle of Delphi. ***"Go, return not die in war"*** can have two opposite meanings, depending on where a missing comma is supposed to be—before or after the word *not.*

In short, when a story from ancient Greek is translated to English, the translated sentences may require proper "repositioning" for an English reader to make better sense of it. For instance, when understanding the syntactic structure of the Greek language and how to "read it" correctly, Plato's second paragraph earlier, to an English reader, should appear as follows:

> (For) the Ocean that was at that time navigable;… and it was possible for travelers of that time to cross from it (*the island of Atlantis*) to the other islands, and from the islands to the whole of the continent over against them which encompasses the veritable ocean…for in front of the mouth which you Greeks call, as you say "the Pillars of Hercules," there lay a continent which was larger than Libya and Asia together.

When seen in this context, the continent across the ocean is no longer the place of origin for Atlanteans but a destination. Here, Plato describes Atlantis's strength by depicting their incredible capability to travel halfway around the world. He explains that via island hopping (most likely from Scotland to the Faroe Islands to Iceland and Greenland), the Atlanteans could reach another great continent on the other side of the Atlantic, one across from the Pillars of Hercules. Which continent is on the opposite side of the Atlantic across from the Strait of Gibraltar? The American continent, of course! It was the American continent that Plato said was larger than Libya and Asia put together and not that of Atlantis as many wrongly had interpreted and even to this day continue to interpret.

As unsettling as it is to some, the revelation that the ancient Greeks knew of the American continent thousands of years before its "discovery" by Christopher Columbus, we must remind ourselves that even much earlier in time, they were fully aware that the Earth was round and not flat, as many European civilizations assumed at the time. The Antikythera Mechanism is a testament to such advanced knowledge.

More evidence from the fourth century BC, though, indicate that the Greeks, along with the Phoenicians and possibly others, knew of the American continent around that time.

The Piri Reis world map, named after its maker, a Turkish admiral and renowned cartographer (1465–1553), drawn in 1513, merely two decades after the discovery of America by Christopher Columbus, depicts the west coast of Africa, Europe, as well as the entire American continent on the Atlantic side. According to Piri Reis, however, his controversial map was based on several other charts, many dating as early as the fourth century BC.

While, by any means, the famous map does not come close to a satellite image, still, it correctly depicts the continents on both sides of the Atlantic, although with one major flaw. It shows South America's horn turning sharply eastward, almost at a ninety-degree angle, as if South America "wraps around" the Atlantic at the bottom of the map. While, of course, some go on to speculate that the horizontal body of that land could be Antarctica's, thus the controversy since Antarctica was not discovered until 300 years later, skeptics point out that Antarctica was never connected to South America.

Although the controversy in Piri Reis's map significantly diminishes without Antarctica in it, the existence of this map still helps reinforce a couple of assumptions made earlier.

If, honestly, Piri Reis borrowed from other ancient maps dating back to the fourth century BC, then unquestionably, this reinforces the suggestion that Plato, at 360 BC, could have been aware of the American continent in order to include it in his story. Moreover, is it possible that the apparent flaw on Piri Reis's map, which most likely also appeared on the much older originals, explains why Plato was under the false impression that the immense continent across from the Pillars of Hercules "encompassed" (wrapped around) the Atlantic Ocean?

Additional clues, though, not only hint that the ancient Greeks were aware of the huge continent across the Atlantic, but as it seems, they were also familiar with the region around the Arctic Circle, in essence, the broken bridge that connects northern Europe and North America. They called this land Hyperborea (Ὑπερβόρεια), a Greek word that literally means "extremely north." Is this possible? After all, Greenland itself, one of the island stops leading to North America, lies at the edge of the Arctic Circle.

While skeptics in the past dismissed this suggestion as an impossible hypothesis, interestingly, the Greeks also documented that Hyperborea was an unspoiled territory so far north, the Sun there shines 24 hours a day. We all know that the only place due north where the Sun never sets, at least six months out of a year, is the region above the Arctic Circle, a territory that is not easily accessible, especially during the winter months. Coincidentally, the poet Pindar (522 BC–443 BC) wrote that "neither by ship nor on foot would you find the marvelous road to the assembly of the Hyperboreans," a statement that further corroborates the inaccessibility of this region.

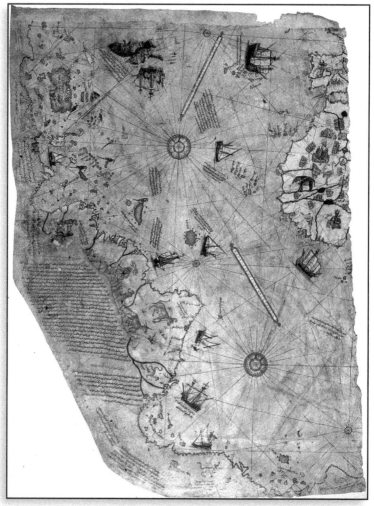

A fragment of the Piri Reis map showing the Central and South American coast on the Atlantic side and the coast of Africa, Portugal, and Spain at the Strait of Gibraltar. The horn of South America curves sharply eastward as if it wraps around the Atlantic at the bottom of the map.

So when considering that this place's location is "extremely north," somewhere where the Sun never sets, and the fact that the terrain of this region is inaccessible by foot or boat (obviously due to the frozen Arctic Ocean), where else on Earth can a place like this be? Can Hyperborea be the figment of vivid imagination, or is it possible that there is some truth to this story, as in other stories brought to us from ancient Greece, which involved real places wrapped in fantastic elements? Such, among others, was the Palace of Knossos, which was associated with the Minotaur (a mythical beast of half man and half-bull); the city of Troy, which was connected with an epic war fought by demigods; and Mount Olympus, which was thought to be occupied by gods. What about Hyperborea, though? Is it possible that the Greeks managed to navigate so far north, or was that knowledge passed down to them from others?

According to historians, more than 4,000 years ago, the Bronze Age Minoans were regularly traveling as far as Scotland and the Orkney Islands to trade goods. If so, is it inconceivable to assume that over several centuries going back and forth, they may have reached Greenland (the edge of Hyperborea), which is just a couple of short island stops away? Moreover, if those ancient navigators managed to get to Greenland via island hopping, can we further assume that they could have gone a bit further and ultimately reached North America, which is just around the corner? If not, how else could Plato have known that a series of islands eventually connect northern Europe to North America? And consequently, can this fact best explain why Plato was under the impression that the enormous continent across from the Pillars of Hercules "encompassed" (encircled) the Atlantic Ocean?

An article published in the *New York Times* on October 10, 1982, talks of an ancient Roman shipwreck and other artifacts found in a bay near Rio de Janeiro. This find, of course, not only substantiates the notion that the Greeks and the Phoenicians followed the Minoans and reached the American continent during the fourth and third century BC, but the Romans had followed them afterwards.

The route to the Arctic Circle (and beyond) known to ancient Greeks as Hyperborea.

Artifacts found in a bay near Rio de Janeiro may mark the wreck of a Roman ship that could have reached Brazil 17 centuries before Portuguese adventurers discovered the region, according to a leading underwater archeologist.

A large accumulation of amphoras, or tall jars, of the type carried by Roman ships in the second century B.C., has been found in Guanabara Bay, 15 miles from Rio de Janeiro, according to the archeologist, Robert Marx, who is a well-known hunter of sunken treasure.

The Portuguese navigator Pedro Alvarez Cabral is generally credited as having been the first European to reach Brazil, in the year 1500. Mr. Marx said yesterday that the Portuguese authorities were trying to block Brazil from issuing him a permit to excavate the wreck he thinks is buried there. Like the 5-Gallon Jerry Can, Amphoras are tall jars tapering to the bottom and usually fitted with twin handles. As described by Mr. Marx, they were to the ancient Greeks, Romans and Phoenicians what the five-gallon jerry can was to mobile units in World War II. They were used to carry wine, oil, water or grain on long voyages…

According to Dr. Harold E. Edgerton of the Massachusetts Institute of Technology, a pioneer in underwater photography who has worked extensively with Mr. Marx, the amphoras are definitive, both as to the age in which they were used and the identity of the users. Reached by telephone, Dr. Edgerton said of Mr. Marx's qualifications, "For my money he is as reliable as they come."[3]

Nearly 40 years later, another discovery and another article published in Armstrong Economics on April 11, 2019, further conveyed that the ancient Romans may have been regular visitors to the New World.

Roman Coins Wash up on Beach in Florida.

There have been discoveries of Roman coins in Japan as well as in North America. There has even been the discovery of a Roman sword in Newfoundland.

Now, a treasure hunter with a metal detector uncovered seven Roman coins that washed up on a beach here in the Tampa region. This is strong evidence that there must have been a

Roman shipwreck off the coast of Tampa or in nearby proximity. These coins are of the 4th century from the era of Constantine. They are bronze and of no particular rarity. In such a condition, they are really worthless. Nevertheless, there certainly seems to have been Roman ships that crossed the Atlantic long before even the Vikings, no less Columbus.[4]

As unbelievable as these revelations may sound to some people, more evidence shows that the Minoans, as well as Plato's Atlanteans before them, were also regular visitors to the New World. Could this have been by mere coincidence? Suppose both cultures were able to travel to America by following the same route. Is it possible to consider that the Atlanteans could have been a proto-Minoan culture that collapsed with the rise of the oceans, only later to reform and recommence as a whole new civilization, at least in the eyes of early historians? If so, is it possible that the rising waters not only washed Atlantis away but also erased the link that connects these two cultures? More evidence later highlights this connection.

To best visualize how an established civilization can break down, only to reemerge centuries or millennia later, we must remind ourselves that a single, relatively insignificant event by comparison (like the fall of Rome, for instance) drove humanity into the dark ages for more than a thousand years. During this period, all past human knowledge somehow seems to have gotten lost, and the Earth went from being a sphere to being flat.

When comparing this somewhat minor incident to that of the rise of the oceans 10,000 years ago (a cataclysm that persisted for centuries and in the process "swallowed" millions of square miles of coastal land and, along with it, all human development), then it is easy to understand the force that literally erased our early history.

A study published in *Science News* (December 4, 2010) titled "Global Sea-Level Rise at the End of the Last Ice Age Interrupted by Rapid Jumps" better explains that after the end of the last Ice Age, from around 17,000 BC through 4,000 BC, sea levels (on average) rose by 1 meter per century. However, the study also indicated that abrupt sea-level jumps marked this gradual rise of the seas at a rate of about 5 meters per century. More precisely, the study showed that the periods between 13,000 BC and 11,000 BC, and between 9,000 BC and 7,000 BC, were characterized by abnormal sea-level rise.

When analyzing the abrupt climatic changes during the last 18,000 years, the time between 9,000 BC and 7,000 BC is of particular interest. As the glaciers began to melt over thousands of years before this period, and the temperatures progressively began to increase with each passing century causing the melting process to accelerate, we can easily presume that this must have been the most active period in sea-level rise. More accurately, the absolute worst period must have been around 8,000 BC and the critical "flood cycle" that led to the Black Sea's flooding, an incident that marked the end of this violent period.

In addition to the glacier meltwater that heavily flowed into the Atlantic, two enormous glacial lakes in North America also burst open, first Lake Agassiz and later Lake Ojibway, and began to drain into the northern Atlantic. Lake Agassiz alone, covering an area larger than all the modern Great Lakes combined (440,000 square kilometers), at times contained more water than all the lakes in the world today. It is estimated that the outburst flood caused by the collapse of Lake Agassiz alone may have been responsible for sea levels to rise globally by as much as 9 feet. The total freshwater outflow from both lakes was so immense that not only quickly raised sea levels worldwide by several feet, but this incident may have ultimately caused the "8.2 kilo-year event" that followed approximately 8,200 years ago (a mini Ice Age that lasted up to four centuries).

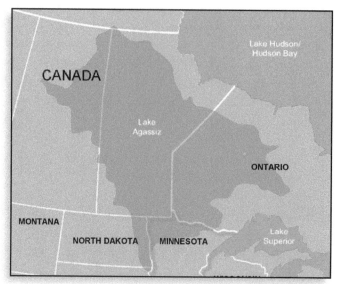

Lake Agassiz covered an area of 440,000 square kilometers, roughly the size of the Black Sea. Major drainage from this lake into the ocean, at around 8,000 BC, had a significant impact on climate, sea level, and early human civilizations.

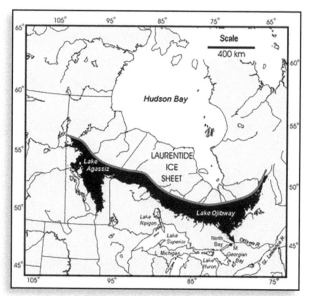

At around 6,000 BC, as the Laurentide Ice Sheet receded, what was left of Lake Agassiz merged with Lake Ojibway. The long lake continued to drain into the sea through the Ottawa River Valley and caused sea levels to rise further.

A recent article published in *Discover* magazine on November 14, 2018, also mentions that an asteroid impact in North America at the end of the last Ice Age caused much glacial water to suddenly pour into the Atlantic. If so, if indeed a meteor struck North America within the same period when Lake Agassiz burst open, then this could very well be the incident behind its sudden collapse:

Massive crater under Greenland's ice points to climate-altering impact in the time of humans.

...Though not as cataclysmic as the dinosaur-killing Chicxulub impact, which carved out a 200-kilometer-wide crater in Mexico about 66 million years ago, the Hiawatha impactor, too, may have left an imprint on the planet's history. ... The impact would have been a spectacle for anyone within 500 kilometers. A white fireball four times larger and three times brighter than the sun would have streaked across the sky. If the object struck an ice sheet, it would have tunneled through to the bedrock, vaporizing water and stone alike in a flash. The resulting explosion packed the energy of 700 1-megaton nuclear bombs, and even an observer hundreds of kilometers away would have experienced a buffeting shock wave, a monstrous thunderclap, and hurricane-force winds. Later, rock debris might have rained down on North America and Europe, and the released steam, a greenhouse gas, could have locally warmed Greenland, melting even more ice.

The news of the impact discovery has reawakened an old debate among scientists who study ancient climate. A massive impact on the ice sheet would have sent meltwater pouring into the Atlantic Ocean—potentially disrupting the conveyor belt of ocean currents and causing temperatures to plunge, especially in the Northern Hemisphere. "What would it mean for species or life at the time? It's a huge open question," says Jennifer Marlon, a paleo-climatologist at Yale University.[5]

All things considered, it was during this period when most coastal civilizations around the planet were lost, including the sunken city in India and that of Atlantis. The continuous, rapid rise of the sea during this period (by an average of 20 to 30 feet per century or more), along with the adverse climatic conditions that accompanied this phenomenon, made it impossible for the remnants of any civilization to reestablish itself.

Another late article published in the *Discover* magazine on August 27, 2019, confirms just that.

Rising Seas Swallowed Countless Archaeological Sites. Scientists Want Them Back.

Whatever you learned in school about how our species spread across the planet is wrong.

For decades, textbooks taught that humans left our ancestral African homeland and spread across the world via the landmasses we know today, reaching Australia less than 50,000 years ago and the Americas a mere 13,500 years ago. But there's a continent-sized gap in our knowledge about our collective past that scientists are only now starting to fill in.

From the North Sea to the island-dotted trop-
ics between Asia and Australia, from the frigid
waters of the Bering Strait to the sunny Arabian
Peninsula, now-submerged coastal landscapes
were exposed and accessible to our ancestors at
multiple times in prehistory, including key periods of human expansion across the globe. The
square mileage of these areas now under the seas
is equal to that of modern North America.

"My own view is that there are certainly sites
out there," says University of York archaeologist
Geoff Bailey. "Some of the areas [that would
have been] most attractive to humans are now
underwater."

The first members of the genus Homo emerged
at roughly the dawn of the Pleistocene, which
began about 2.6 million years ago and ended with
the final drips of the last great glacial melt, about
12,000 years ago. It is, essentially, the epoch of
human evolution. By its end, only one species of
human remained—us—and we had settled and
thrived on every continent except Antarctica.

For 95 percent of the time that humans have
existed, sea levels have been lower than they are
now, usually by about 130 feet. At their lowest,
they were about 400 feet lower, globally, than
they are today.[6]

Essentially, only closer to 7,000 BC, when the ocean levels finally
began to stabilize, human life once more began to return to normal.
Coastal sites no longer had to be abandoned for higher ground, and
between 6,000 BC and 5,000 BC, we begin to see signs of human
activity closer to the sea once more. Is it a mere coincidence that our

"recorded" history happens to start around this time? Is it true that early humans were too primitive to leave traces of their existence behind, or the early pages of our history (as more evidence now shows) were "washed away" by the Great Flood of the last Ice Age? After all, it seems that as soon as the adverse climatic conditions receded, it did not take long for humans to thrive once again.

Consequently, Plato's Atlanteans, now called the Minoans by modern historians (due to lack of precursor evidence), once more became that great seafaring civilization they once were.

Indeed, an article posted in the UW News (University of Washington) on May 14, 2013, indicated that a recent study not only identified the Minoans as the first major European civilization, but DNA analysis further confirmed that their civilization arose from the same proto-Minoan culture already living on the island of Crete for thousands of years.

DNA Analysis Unearths Origins of Minoans, the First Major European Civilization.

DNA analysis is unearthing the origins of the Minoans, who some 5,000 years ago established the first advanced Bronze Age civilization in present-day Crete. The findings suggest they arose from an ancestral Neolithic population that had arrived in the region more than 4,000 years earlier.

The British archeologist Sir Arthur Evans in the early 1900s named the Minoans after a legendary Greek king, Minos. Based on similarities between Minoan artifacts and those from Egypt and Libya, Evans proposed that the Minoan civilization founders migrated into the area from North Africa. Since then, other archaeologists have suggested that the Minoans may have come from other regions, possibly Turkey, the Balkans, or the Middle East.

Now, a team of researchers in the United States and Greece has used mitochondrial DNA analysis of Minoan skeletal remains to determine the likely ancestors of these ancient people.

Results published May 14 in Nature Communications suggest that the Minoan civilization arose from the population already living in Bronze Age Crete. The findings indicate that these people probably were descendants of the first humans to reach Crete more than 9,000 years ago, and that they have the greatest genetic similarity with modern European populations.[7]

So as we are told, not only the Minoans ascended from the same proto-Minoan culture, but as it seems, "the apple did not fall far from the tree." Just as the proto-Minoans (or Atlanteans if you prefer) managed to leave their genetic fingerprint on the American continent thousands of years earlier (more evidence on that later), the Minoans also traveled and traded outside the Mediterranean and often brought goods from the New World, as some evidence shows.

Several clues in North America, as well as on the island of Santorini, confirm that during the Bronze Age, the Minoans not only were heavily mining copper from the area around Lake Superior, but they were regularly carrying tobacco and other herbs from the Americas back to Santorini. Many ancient copper mines around the Great Lakes and primarily in the upper peninsula of Michigan are a testament of those days. More than five thousand shallow mines, up to 20 feet in depth, were discovered within an area roughly 200 kilometers long by 10 kilometers wide. Carbon dating of artifacts found around these mines revealed that the mines were active during the Bronze Age, between 2,470 BC and 1,050 BC. A carbon 14 testing of wood remains found inside sockets of copper artifacts on Isle Royale and nearby Keweenaw Peninsula (a region filled with copper mine pits) indicated that some mines in that area were in use between 3,700 BC and 5,000 BC, if not earlier.

A conservative estimate indicates that around 3,000 BC, as many as five hundred thousand tons of copper were extracted from the upper peninsula of Michigan, an undertaking that cannot be clearly explained by mainstream historians or archaeologists. Not only no one in the New World at that time could have extracted and used the copper, but no significant copper remnants were ever found in the Americas to account for the missing ore. So while today's researchers theorize that some ancient European civilization may have been the one to have utilized the precious metal, the only Bronze Age culture at the time capable of navigating to the Americas were the post-Atlantean Minoans.

More evidence, however, ties the Minoans to the New World. Ancient tools left behind at Lake Superior match those of the Minoans found in other European mines. Also, the type of copper extracted from North America, when chemically tested, closely matches the Minoan product.

Evidence that connects the Minoans to the Americas, though, also exist on the island of Santorini. Archaeological excavations on the island revealed that the Minoans were also importing tobacco from North America. More precisely, an excavation in the ancient city of Akrotiri, near what was a merchant's house, revealed that a tobacco beetle indigenous to America was buried under the volcanic ash of the 1,600 BC eruption. As the tobacco beetle, *Lasioderma serricorne*, was indigenous only to America at the time, and historically tobacco was not introduced to Europeans until around AD 1518 (nearly 3,000 years later), this find further reinforces the suggestion that the Minoans were importing tobacco along with copper from the New World.

This revelation solves yet another historical puzzle. It explains how, during this period, ancient Egyptians obtained tobacco and other spices native to America. Several early tests on Egyptian mummies revealed that some plants and herbs, including tobacco, used during the mummification process, were indigenous to Central America. Interestingly, the same type of beetle that was discovered in Santorini, a sort of "pest of stored tobacco," was also found inside the mummy of Ramses II (1,213 BC) and King Tutankhamen's tomb (1,323 BC).

In 1992, more tests by German scientists on several mummies exposed remnants of hashish, tobacco, and cocaine on their hair, skin, and bones. The results were a huge surprise. Unlike the hashish that historically originates in Asia, tobacco and coca were strictly New World plants at the time of mummification. To be sure that the results were not tainted somehow, or most likely, to allow themselves to step outside this controversial discovery, the German team hired an independent lab to redo these tests. The independent lab found precisely the same substances. Out of the hundreds of mummies they tested, including Ramses II, they found nicotine traces on at least a third of them. This discovery leaves no doubt that not only the ancient Egyptians needed a large supply of tobacco, but as it appears, it was the enterprising Minoans that were regularly supplying them with it.

The best proof to connect the Minoans and their ancestors to the Americas, though, other than copper, tobacco, and other plants indigenous to America, is DNA evidence. DNA analysis shows that in their endeavors to the Americas, the same proto-Minoan culture (one Plato referred to as Atlanteans) left their genetic fingerprint behind.

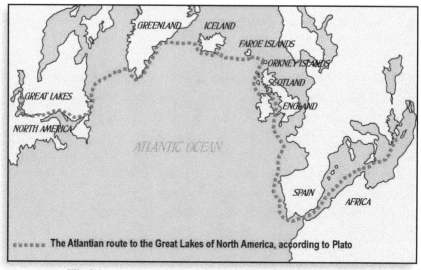

The Atlantian route to the Great Lakes of North America, according to Plato

The Minoan route to North America during the Bronze Age

For the longest time, geneticists wondered and debated how haplogroup X, an eastern Mediterranean gene, migrated to America thousands of years before the Europeans discovered the American continent. More specifically, how did some tribes in North America, and suspiciously those that originated around the Great Lakes, like the Ojibwa and Chippewa Indians, found to carry this gene while other tribes further away didn't? The mystery deepened when scientists suggested that the Mediterranean haplogroup X could have "mutated" among the North American tribes as early as 12,000 years ago.

For those not familiar with genetics, according to the International Society of Genetic Genealogy, a haplogroup is a genetic population group of people who share a common ancestor on either their paternal or maternal line. In short, each race around the planet is categorized by scientists according to their particular DNA haplogroup. For example, all American Indians carry haplogroups A, B, C, and D. As haplogroups A, C, and D are also found primarily in Asia and B mainly in China and Japan, anthropologists had speculated long ago that these four haplogroups traveled to North America during a glacier period when continents were once connected by ice.

A more recent study, though, on specific Native American tribes around the Great Lakes, like the Iroquois Indians and a few others, revealed that in addition to the above haplogroups that scientists had expected to find, they were also found to carry haplogroup X.

This discovery came as a big surprise because haplogroup X originates from an area that incorporates the eastern Mediterranean, Greece, Turkey, the Palestinian territories, Syria, Jordan, Lebanon, Cyprus, Israel, and northeast Africa.

Indeed, an article published in the PMC Journal (US National Library of Medicine National Institutes of Health) in December 1998 also concluded that "some Native American founders were of Caucasian ancestry."

mtDNA haplogroup X: An ancient link between Europe/Western Asia and North America?

On the basis of comprehensive RFLP analysis, it has been inferred that approximately 97% of Native American mtDNAs belong to one of four major founding mtDNA lineages, designated haplogroups "A"-"D." It has been proposed that a fifth mtDNA haplogroup (haplogroup X) represents a minor founding lineage in Native Americans. Unlike haplogroups A-D, haplogroup X is also found at low frequencies in modern European populations. To investigate the origins, diversity, and continental relationships of this haplogroup, we performed mtDNA high-resolution RFLP and complete control region (CR) sequence analysis on 22 putative Native American haplogroup X and 14 putative European haplogroup X mtDNAs. The results identified a consensus haplogroup X motif that characterizes our European and Native American samples. Among Native Americans, haplogroup X appears to be essentially restricted to northern Amerindian groups, including the Ojibwa, the Nuu-Chah-Nulth, the Sioux, and the Yakima, although we also observed this haplogroup in the Na-Dene-speaking Navajo. Median network analysis indicated that European and Native American haplogroup X mtDNAs, although distinct, nevertheless are distantly related to each other. Time estimates for the arrival of X in North America are 12,000-36,000 years ago, depending on the number of assumed founders, thus supporting the conclusion that the peoples harboring haplogroup X were among the original founders of Native American populations. To date, haplogroup X has not been unambiguously identified in Asia, raising the possibility that some Native American founders were of Caucasian ancestry.[8]

Consequently if eastern Mediterranean people somehow made it to America 10,000 years ago, why did only tribes around the Great Lakes carry this gene? Moreover, how did Mediterranean people manage the trip to North America? Is it possible, as many anthropologists today suggest, that 12,000 years ago, they traveled to America by foot while ice still connected the Asian and American continents at the Bering Strait? After all, as we are told, this is how haplogroups A, B, C, and D crossed over to the Americas. A big problem with this theory, though, is that en route from the Middle East to America, the furthest region east of the Mediterranean to carry small traces of haplogroup X is that of the Altai Republic in Russia. No traces of haplogroup X (or another variation of X) exist further east of that region. And while most scientists continue to hold onto the Bering Strait hypothesis, no one can provide a conclusive explanation for the lack of haplogroup X in the enormous void between southern Russia and the greater region of the Great Lakes.

Of course, some supported an earlier theory called the Solutrean/ Clovis hypothesis, which suggests the crossing was not made through the Bering Strait, but instead, those carrying haplogroup X crossed over to America on an ice sheet that partially connected Europe with North America. Oddly enough, this scenario suggests that out of the ten distinct haplogroups present in northern Europe at the time (H, V, J, HV, U, T, UK, X, W, and I), conveniently, only haplogroup X managed the trip to America. The model in this particular hypothesis also required that the early travelers, 12,000 years ago, crossed over to the Americas in small watercrafts constructed out of animal skins and used survival skills similar to Inuit people, not exactly the trades of Mediterranean culture. Considering all this, another study done in 2008 using relevant oceanographic data pointed out that such crossing conditions were not favorable, and the majority of scientists afterward dismissed the Solutrean hypothesis.

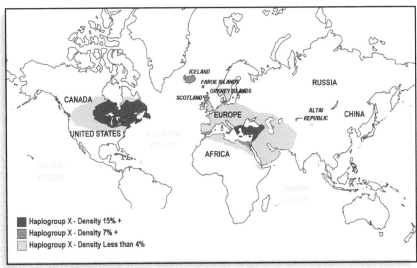

According to mtDNA maps, the highest concentration of haplogroup X away from the eastern Mediterranean (the place of origin of haplogroup X) is found around North America's Great Lakes. Incidentally, and just as Plato mentioned, high traces of haplogroup X also exist around the Strait of Gibraltar, Scotland, Orkney Islands, Faroe Islands, and Iceland (every island stop from Europe to the New World).

Therefore, the mystery of how haplogroup X made it to North America remains. If somehow the path to America was open from either direction (via the Bering Strait or the North Atlantic), and any European gene could follow haplogroup X to the New World by foot, how do we explain that only one Caucasian/Mediterranean gene (out of at least a dozen) made this trip 12,000 years ago, when by contrast, on the opposite side, every one of the four Asian haplogroups sequentially managed to follow each other to America through the Bering Strait? Conversely, if haplogroup X did not enter America via the Atlantic, how do we explain the fact that elevated traces of haplogroup X "strangely" exist in Scotland, Faroe Islands, and Iceland, practically all the "island stops" on the way to North America from Europe. We must also not ignore that mtDNA maps show that the highest concentrations of haplogroup X exist on the Atlantic side, around Newfoundland and the Great Lakes, and not in Alaska or alongside the west coast, where according to science, haplogroup X infiltrated America.

While mainstream academia and critics to this day still insist on the Bering Strait hypothesis, a scientific article published in 2015 in *PaleoAmerica* (a journal of early human migration and dispersal) may have otherwise conclusively settled this debate. A report with the title "Does Mitochondrial Haplogroup X Indicate Ancient Trans-Atlantic Migration to the Americas? A Critical Re-Evaluation" explained that the variety of haplogroup X2 found among native Americans has an entirely different lineage than that of X2 found in the Altai Republic. In short, as the two lineages were found to be completely unrelated, it was determined that haplogroup X did not migrate to North America via the Altai Republic or the Bering Strait. More surprisingly, the report further concluded that the presence of X2a in America, in addition to X2, has been cited as evidence of not just one but two separate transatlantic migrations during our prehistory.

Does Mitochondrial Haplogroup X Indicate Ancient Trans-Atlantic Migration to the Americas? A Critical Re-Evaluation.

The X2a (and the related, rare haplogroup X2g) is a uniquely North American haplogroup, found at the highest frequencies in Great Lakes populations and at lower frequencies in the Plains and Pacific Northwest. It appears to be completely absent in populations from Central and South America (Perego et al. 2009). Its presence in pre-European contact skeletal remains confirms that it was not the result of post-1492 admixture (Bolnick and Smith 2007; Malhi and Smith 2002; Rasmussen et al. 2015). However, unlike the other American mitochondrial haplogroups (A–D), which have clear parental haplotypes persisting in contemporary Siberian populations, there is no clear record of the evolutionary history of X2a in any population (Fernandes et al. 2012; Reidla et al. 2003). X2a's "grand-parental" haplogroup, X2, is found throughout, at low levels today throughout much of the world, including in the Near East (where X is more common and therefore thought to have initially evolved), South Caucasus, Europe, Siberia, Central Asia, and North Africa (Reidla et al. 2003). It is important to note that while the Altai people in southern Siberia exhibit X2 (Derenko et al. 2001), their lineages are not ancestral to those of North Americans, and the presence of X2 there today appears to be the result of recent gene flow from the west (Reidla et al. 2003). Thus, the intermediate lineages linking X2 and X2a appear to have been lost in contemporary populations or are so rare that they have not yet been well studied. We might expect to find them in ancient populations, but our temporal and spatial coverage of ancient populations is still quite sparse. Despite—or perhaps because of—this gap in the phylogeographic record for haplogroup X2, the presence of X2a in North America has been cited as evidence for two different trans-Atlantic migrations before European contact.[9]

So before allowing for religious beliefs to become reasonable theories, like the Mormon hypothesis, which supports the notion that 10,000 years ago, Israelites "appeared" in America with God's "assistance," is it time perhaps to give Plato's testament another closer look? Unlike other "scientific," nonscientific, and religious theories, Plato's explanation offers the most compelling evidence of how haplogroup X arrived at the New World in a contained environment.

For the Ocean that was at that time navigable;... and it was possible for travelers of that time to cross from it (*the island of Atlantis*) to the other islands, and from the islands to the whole of the continent over against them which encompasses the veritable ocean...

Plato's claim that Atlanteans had made it to the New World with boats via island hopping not only explains why other haplogroups were not able to follow X, but this further illustrates why heavy traces of haplogroup X also exist on every island stop from Europe to North America.

Indeed, in the following paragraph, Plato further clarifies how much influence the Atlanteans had over these islands and over the continent itself:

For all that we have here, lying within the mouth of which we speak, is evidently a haven having a narrow entrance; but that yonder is a real ocean, and the land surrounding it may most rightly be called, in the fullest and truest sense, a continent. *Now in this island of Atlantis there existed a confederation of kings, of great and marvelous power, which held sway over all the island, and over many other islands also and parts of the continent.*

Once again, when interpreting the above text, the main emphasis must be placed on the paragraph's first and last sentence (*highlighted in bold italic*). While these two sentences convey the topic, the middle sentence, in this case, provides the supporting details.

In this paragraph, Plato depicts Atlantis as an idyllic place with a narrow entrance somewhere within the Mediterranean Sea (*"lying within the mouth of which we speak"*). He then explains that the mighty Atlanteans not only had great power over their island, but they *"held sway"* over several more islands (the Orkney Islands, Faroe Islands, Iceland, Greenland, etc.) leading to the continent across the ocean, as well as over parts of the continent itself. Finally, in the second sentence in the clause, the supporting sentence, in this case, he further maintains and confirms that *"yonder"* (outside the Mediterranean), there is a *"real ocean,"* and the enormous land surrounding this ocean, he explains, is so vast it *"may most rightly be called, in the fullest and truest sense, a continent."*

When comparing Plato's account to the earlier map, is there a doubt that he offers the most convincing explanation yet how haplogroup X migrated to the New World, and why heavy traces of X also exist on every island stop from Europe to the Great Lakes of North America?

While this explanation appears to be more plausible in comparison to others, we must not ignore the fact that when the original human migration scenarios were first proposed to explain the presence of haplogroup X in America, the mainstream academia assumed that 10,000 years ago, humans were still behaving as hunters and gatherers. With that in mind, it is no wonder that Plato's story was immediately dismissed as a myth.

Of course, recent archaeological discoveries, like that of Gobekli Tepe in Turkey (10,000 BC) and the sunken city off the coast of West India (8,000 BC), not only prove that humans had advanced much earlier, but they could have plausibly reached North America. Unlike other mainstream theories, Plato's story places haplogroup X in America in the correct chronology and explains how, in a contained environment, it arrived at the Great Lakes. By the way, let us not forget that 11,000 years ago, with the ocean levels at least 400 feet lower, there was so much more landmass between Scotland, Iceland, and Greenland that island hopping to North America could not have been more difficult than crisscrossing the Mediterranean. Any competent prehistoric Mediterranean navigator, who could travel as far as Scotland, ultimately could have developed the skills to navigate to North America as well.

Indeed! An article published in the National Geographic on February 17, 2010, revealed more than that. The title of the article is "Primitive Humans Conquered Sea, Surprising Finds Suggest." Prehistoric axes found on a Greek island suggest that seafaring existed in the Mediterranean more than 100,000 years earlier than previously thought.

Primitive Humans Conquered Sea, Surprising Finds Suggest.

Two years ago a team of U.S. and Greek archaeologists were combing a gorge on the island of Crete in Greece, hoping to find tiny stone tools employed by seafaring people who had plied nearby waters some 11,000 years ago.

Instead, in the midst of the search, Providence College archaeologist Thomas Strasser and his team came across a whopping surprise—a sturdy 5-inch-long (13-centimeter-long) hand ax.

Knapped from a cobble of local quartz stone, the rough-looking tool resembled hand axes discovered in Africa and mainland Europe and used by human ancestors until about 175,000 years ago. This stone tool technology, which could have been useful for smashing bones and cutting flesh, had been relatively static for over a million years.

Crete has been surrounded by vast stretches of sea for some five million years. The discovery of the hand ax suggests that people besides technologically modern humans—possibly Homo heidelbergensis—island-hopped across the Mediterranean tens of thousands of millennia earlier than expected.

Many researchers have hypothesized that the early humans of this time period were not capable of devising boats or navigating across open water. But the new discoveries hint that these human ancestors were capable of much more sophisticated behavior than their relatively simple stone tools would suggest.

"I was flabbergasted," said Boston University archaeologist and stone-tool expert Curtis Runnels. "The idea of finding tools from this very early time period on Crete was about as believable as finding an iPod in King Tutankhamen's tomb."[10]

As difficult as it is for some people to accept that a prehistoric Mediterranean culture discovered the New World, additional physical evidence confirms that a Caucasian race did visit North America nearly 10,000 years ago.

The Kennewick Man is the name given to the skeletal remains of a prehistoric man found on a bank of the Columbia River in Kennewick, Washington, on July 28, 1996. Will Thomas and David Deacy accidentally discovered the skull while they were attending an annual event. Later, a team of professionals recovered 350 additional skeletal pieces, making the Kennewick Man the most complete prehistoric skeleton ever found. Interestingly, while scientists initially thought the remains belonged to a Native Indian from the nineteenth century, a radiocarbon dating conducted by the University of California at Riverside concluded that the skeleton was approximately 9,800 years old. Even more incredibly, when forensic archaeologist James Chatters further studied the bones and especially the skeleton's cranium features, he concluded that they belonged to a Caucasoid male about 68 inches (or 173 centimeters) tall.

> The man lacks definitive characteristics of the classic mongoloid stock to which modern Native Americans belong. The skull is dolichocranic (cranial index 73.8) rather than brachycranic, the face narrow and prognathous rather than broad and flat. Cheek bones recede slightly and lack an inferior zygomatic projection; the lower rim of the orbit is even with the upper. Other features are a long, broad nose that projects markedly from the face and high, round orbits. The mandible is V-shaped, with a pronounced, deep chin. Many of these characteristics are definitive of modern-day Caucasoid peoples, while others, such as the orbits are typical of neither race.[11]

Additional studies, since, were conducted to determine the origin of the Kennewick Man, with some speculating he must have been of Asian ancestry. Unfortunately, though, when a sample was extracted from the skeleton to determine—once and for all—the origin, age, and race of the remains, early DNA results came back inconclusive.

More recent work on the remains by Douglas Owsley, though, a physical anthropologist at the Smithsonian Institution's National Museum of History, further concluded that the Kennewick Man's ancestors did not originate in northern Asia like those of most Native Americans who are believed to have crossed from Asia to Alaska about 11,000 years ago. Even when comparing the skull of Kennewick Man to a typical Polynesian skull (as some theorized Polynesia may have been his place of origin), certain cranium features, like the lower jawbone, still support the initial diagnosis that the remains belong to a Caucasoid.

Even if the Kennewick Man ultimately was found to be Polynesian, his presence in North America still corroborates Plato's claim that ten millennia ago, another Mediterranean culture of skillful navigators could sail to the New World. Clearly, following the much longer coastline from Polynesia to North America presents far greater challenges than crossing over to the Americas from Europe via the North Atlantic.

Ultimately, another somewhat controversial genome study published in the journal *Nature* in 2015 concluded that the Kennewick Man was not of Asian origin as some people previously speculated. While the study agreed with all other anthropologists that the Kennewick Man's unique skeletal remains did not match those of other Native Americans, the final analysis concluded that his genome data found him closer to modern Native Americans than any other group (thus the controversy). In December 2016, against Douglas Owsley's and several other scientists' appeals, President Obama signed legislation that would allow the Kennewick Man to be returned to his homeland and laid to rest. In February of 2017, dozens of boxes holding the

Kennewick Man's remains were retrieved by nearly thirty members of the Yakama, Umatilla, Nez Perce, Colville, and Wanapum tribes.

Was this a politically correct decision from the federal government to appease the native tribes in the area where the Kennewick Man was originally found? After all, for 20 years, they were claiming ancestral relationship and asking for his repatriation under the Native American Graves Protection and Repatriation Act (NAGPRA).

What is extremely important to mention in this case, those who conceded to label the Kennewick Man, a Native American, ignored that the study also revealed that his haplogroup consisted of Q-M3 (a North American haplogroup) and X2a (a variation of the Mediterranean Caucasoid haplogroup that migrated to North America 11,000 years BP). In other words, if the Mediterranean ancestors of Kennewick Man had arrived at the New World a thousand years earlier, as Plato suggested, then the Kennewick Man is the descendant of a Mediterranean male with a Native American female. And yes, since the Kennewick Man was born in North America several centuries after his ancestors' arrival, his genome test would undoubtedly show him to have close ties to the New World. However, his haplogroup X, as well as in this case his skeletal remains, would point to his Caucasian origin, as Douglas Owsley originally suggested.

The Kennewick Man's remarkable discovery (as well as the later DNA study) not only confirm Plato's claim that a race of prehistoric Mediterranean people traveled to the New World 10,000 years ago, but this find reinforces the conclusion that a few millennia later, they were followed by their successors—the post-Atlantean Minoans.

The Minoan presence in America during the Bronze Age not only helps account for the missing copper around Lake Superior but can explain the Caucasian "sightings" in Central America reported by the Mayan Indians.

The Mayans, one of Central America's greatest and most mysterious civilizations, were established around 2,000 BC and are known to have been the dominant power in Central America for more than two millennia. While, on the surface, we know them to be expert architects and masters of astronomy, in truth, very little is known about these people and their civilization. Author Charles Gallenkamp, in his book *Maya: The Riddle and Rediscovery of a Lost Civilization*, wrote,

> Regardless of everything scientists have learned about the Maya so far, we constantly encounter unanswered questions. No one has satisfactorily explained where or when Maya civilization originated, or how it evolved in an environment so hostile to human habitation. We have almost no reliable information on the origin of their calendar, hieroglyphic writing, and mathematical system; nor do we understand countless details pertaining to sociopolitical organization, religion, economic structure, and everyday life. Even the shattering catastrophe leading to the sudden abandonment of their greatest cities during the ninth century AD—one of the most baffling archaeological mysteries ever uncovered—is still deeply shrouded in conjecture.[12]

Chronologically, the Mayan civilization emerged during the Bronze Age, while the Minoans heavily mined copper from around Lake Superior. Is this timing just an unrelated coincidence or a clue worth following?

While the Mayans are not known to have traveled as far north as Lake Superior, and they did not encounter the Minoans there, they depicted their god Kukulkan as a Caucasian person with white hair about 6 feet tall.

The Mayans explain that Kukulkan came from the sea, and when it was time for him to leave, once again, he departed back to the sea with a promise that one day, he would return. According to them, Kukulkan taught them how to organize and manage their civilization and taught them agriculture, medicine, and architecture. Who Kukulkan was and why the Mayans portrayed him as a White man is anyone's guess. Or is there an explanation for that? Is it possible that Kukulkan was a Bronze Age visitor to the Great Lakes who, in search of more wealth and opportunity, may have traveled farther south to Central America and ultimately helped or inspired the local tribes to organize? Certainly, Kukulkan's arrival from the sea and his appearance are highly suspicious.

If not a Bronze Age visitor, who was this Caucasian person that the Mayans attributed their culture to? Although no one will ever know for sure, one thing is certain: When the Mayans met the Spanish conquistadors for the "first time," not only did they mistake them for gods, but they thought the Spanish arrival was the return of Kukulkan. Once again, why would the Mayans think the European settlers were gods? Is it possible that an earlier Minoan visit had something to do with that presumption?

If the Minoans were traveling back and forth to North America for more than a thousand years, is there any doubt that they could have traveled further south until, ultimately, they reached Central America? Some evidence, as well as Mayan testimony, confirms this suggestion.

In 1966, Manfred Metcalf, a civilian employee of Fort Benning in Georgia, was gathering stones for a barbeque pit when he discovered a flat, square-shaped, five-pound stone with strange symbols engraved on it. This rock was later named the Metcalf Stone. Thinking that the symbols on the stone could have been some form of Indian writing, Mr. Metcalf presented the stone to Dr. Joseph Mahan Jr., an expert in Yuchi Indian dialect and director of the Columbus Museum of Arts and Crafts. When the stone was presented to him, Dr. Mahan had been primarily studying the Yuchi Indians, a tribe in the region that was racially and linguistically different from all other Indians in North America.

In 1968, when Dr. Mahan completed his studies on the stone, he forwarded a cast copy to Cyrus Gordon at Brandeis University. To everyone's surprise, Mr. Gordon concluded that the markings on the stone matched characters used by the Minoans 3,500 years earlier on the island of Crete.

In effect, if Mr. Gordon's assessment is correct and the inscription on the Metcalf Stone is Minoan, this not only reinforces the notion that the Bronze Age Minoans traveled as far south as the state of Georgia but also raises a valid question of whether there is a connection between the Minoans and the Yuchi Indians in the area, a tribe of "Indians" like no other. Furthermore, the Minoan presence in the southeastern United States also suggests that the Minoans may have traveled farther south and maybe all the way to Central America—not just once but repeatedly. After all, let us not forget that the tobacco that Minoans were regularly carrying back to Santorini is known to have been native to the southwestern United States, Mexico, and parts of South America.

An ancient Yucatan manuscript from the town of Motul further supports this conclusion. It describes a time when the Mayans worshipped a heavenly god and creator of all things until a long-bearded Caucasian prince named Kukulkan arrived from the sea. Contrary to earlier Mayan religious beliefs and practices, he brought the "dark side" to their civilization. In his book *Fair Gods and Feathered Serpents*, T. J. O'Brien noted the following:

> Originally a god had been worshiped here who was the creator of all things, and who had his dwelling in heaven, but that great prince named Kukulkan with a multitude of people had come from a foreign country, that he and his people

were idolaters, and from that time the inhabitants of this land also began to practice idolatry,
to perform bloody sacrificial rites, to burn copal,
and the like.[13]

Kukulkan and his "multitude of people" (his crewmates, perhaps?)
were idol worshippers, and he frequently commanded sacrificial
ceremonies to be enacted in his name. Among other bizarre sacrifices, he often asked that young virgins be thrown 65 feet down
into the water well of Chichen Itza to take messages to the gods of
the underworld. During the twentieth century, when the well was
dredged, researchers found several remains of women, children, and
men whose bodies had been discarded in the enormous well.

The same manuscript further explains that even after the long-
bearded man's departure, the Mayans continued to build temples
to his name and perform human sacrifices to honor him. Strangely,
figures of bearded men, an uncommon facial characteristic among
Central American Indians, were also carved in various stone monuments, including one on the wall of Chichen Itza's ball court. Who
was this bearded man? Is it possible that Kukulkan was a Minoan
perpetrator who demanded human offerings? And if so, were the
Minoans at all known to have practiced human sacrifices? Surprisingly,
the answer is yes. Recent archaeological excavations and evidence
from three different sites on the island of Crete suggest that the
Minoans indeed sacrificed humans. The three areas are Anemospilia,
in a building near Mount Juktas that is interpreted as a temple; in a
sanctuary complex at Fournou Korifi in South-Central Crete; and at
Knossos, in a building known as the North House.

So if the Minoans made it to Central America and, in the process,
they were mistaken as gods, is it possible then to assume that the
dreadful tradition that plagued the Mayan civilization could have
been a tradition that was introduced to them by another culture (and
vice versa)? Is it possible that some Mayan practices and objects
from Central America were taken back to Crete and displayed by the

Minoans as well? For example, under a closer examination, the elaborate headpiece with the long colorful feathers in a famous Minoan fresco (named "Prince of Lilies") could be, in effect, a depiction of a "souvenir" brought back from the New World. If anything, it profoundly resembles a helmet piece usually worn by Mayan priests rather than Minoan royalty. While, traditionally, we see similar headgear as a traditional piece of attire in Mayan art, this distinct piece will not be seen again in other Minoan illustrations. More particularly, all other headpieces depicted in Minoan art appear to be slim, elegant, and ringlike hair straps. Is it possible then that this particular headpiece could be of Mayan origin? Was it a trophy perhaps brought from the New World? The fact is, in both depictions, the long colorful feathers are identical, the material the helmets are made of appears to be woven in the same fashion, and "coincidentally," at the front of both helmets, there is an ornament that leaps out forward. Likewise, just as the servant does behind the Mayan priest, the Minoan similarly salutes with his right fist on his chest, all while his left hand is holding or pulling a rope (what or who is this rope tight around to we will never know).

(Left) A Mayan priest's depiction with a typical attire and an elaborate headpiece with long colorful feathers (1787 illustration by Ricardo Almendariz of a stucco relief at Palenque).
(Right) A Minoan fresco from Crete, labeled by archaeologists as "The prince of Lilies," depicts someone wearing a matching headpiece.

Soon after the Minoan demise at around 1,500 BC, various artifacts and inscriptions from other Middle Eastern cultures found in North America confirm that others eventually took notice and ultimately followed the Minoan footsteps to the Americas. It is believed that the Mycenaean Greeks, along with the Phoenicians, followed the Minoans next. Like the Minoans, the Greeks also left behind their own small relics and other clues to reveal their presence in the New World. The fact that the most western island of Faroe Islands still bears the name "Mykines" (Mycenae in Greek) implies that the Mycenaean Greeks, as the Atlanteans and Minoans before them, may have indeed visited North America via island hopping. By the way, out of four island stops, this was the second stop to North America from Scotland.

After the Mycenaean Greeks, the Phoenicians, who came to the New World just a few centuries after the Minoans, were also an enter-prising maritime trading culture that thrived around the eastern Mediterranean between 1,500 BC and 300 BC. Very much like the Minoans, they could travel outside the Strait of Gibraltar, where they usually traded goods as far as the Azores Islands and alongside the African coast on the Atlantic side. The Phoenicians are also known to have circumnavigated Africa, so for them, a trip to America via "island hopping" would not be an improbable suggestion. Indeed, Paleo-Hebrew inscriptions found in North America also suggest that the Phoenicians made it to the New World, and while there, it is possible that they met the Mayans. The Bat Creek Stone, found in a burial mound in Tennessee, was inscribed with Paleo-Hebrew letter-ing and dates between the first and second centuries AD.

Another find that may be placing the Phoenicians in the Americas is the petroglyphs inscribed on the Dighton Rock found in Berkley, Massachusetts. In 1783, Ezra Stiles, then president of Yale College, identified the writing on Dighton Rock as being Hebrew—a lan-guage also commonly used by the Phoenicians. At the time, the Phoenicians and Israelites were cohabitants of the land of Canaan and were so closely intertwined that they often intermarried and worshipped common Canaanite gods.

The Bat Creek Stone, found in a burial mound in Tennessee, was inscribed with Paleo-Hebrew lettering and dates between the first and second centuries AD. In June 2010, the stone underwent scanning electron microscopy (SEM) examination by American Petrographic Services at the McClung Museum on the campus of the University of Tennessee. After examining the stone's inscribed grooves and outer weathering rind using standard and scanning electron microscopy (SEM) and researching the historical documentation, the team of Scott Wolter and Richard Stehly of American Petrographic Services concluded that the inscription is "consistent with many hundreds of years of weathering in a wet earth mound comprised of soil and hard red clay" and it "can be no younger than when the bodies of the deceased were buried inside the mound."

The Dighton Rock found in Berkley, Massachusetts. More than a dozen theories have been proposed since Ezra Stiles (1727–1795) identified the writing as Paleo-Hebrew, a language also commonly used by the Phoenicians. The inscriptions on the rock have been since attributed to Phoenicians, Vikings, Native Americans, Portuguese, and others.

Is it possible that the Minoan and, most importantly, the Phoenician presence in the southeastern United States can explain why some Indian tribes in this region, like the Cherokee, proclaim Jewish genealogy? Although initially those claims and beliefs were highly questioned by skeptics, it is worth mentioning that recent DNA tests revealed that Cherokee roots include Greek, Phoenician, Carthaginian, Egyptian, and Hebrew lineages. Indeed, the Phoenician lineage is so strong among the Cherokee Indians that some DNA scientists now say that genetically, the Cherokee are Middle Easterners with a high level of European DNA in them.

Just like the Phoenicians influenced the Cherokee Indians, is it possible to assume that in their endeavors at the New World, before their demise, the Minoans met and helped the Mayans establish their own civilization? If so, can we further assume that the Phoenicians perhaps offered their contribution a few centuries later? In fact, if not the Minoans, could the Phoenicians be the white, long-bearded men the Mayans talked about? Lastly, does this alleged interaction in any way explain why Mayan architecture appears to be a hybrid of Minoan and Mesopotamian structures?

(Left) The Northern Temple located on the north side of Chichen Itza's ball court, typically represented the heavens. This is also referred to as the Temple of the Bearded Man because of a relief inside showing a figure with facial hair, a rarity among Mesoamerican archeological sites. (Right) The bearded man on the wall of the Northern Temple.

While several Mayan buildings undoubtedly carry Minoan features and characteristics, the Mayans (and later the Aztecs) are also known for their step pyramids, an architectural element that best matches Middle Eastern architecture, especially the ziggurats of ancient Mesopotamia. Maybe a Phoenician influence could best explain that. In his 1871 book *Ancient America*, John Denison Baldwin wrote,

> The known enterprise of the Phoenician race, and this ancient knowledge of America, so variously expressed, strongly encourage the hypothesis that the people called Phoenicians came to this continent, established colonies in the region where ruined cities are found, and filled it with civilized life. It is argued that they made voyages on the "great exterior ocean," and that such navigators must have crossed the Atlantic; and it is added that symbolic devices similar to those of the Phoenicians are found in the American ruins, and that an old tradition of the native Mexicans and Central Americans described the first civilizers as "bearded white men," who "came from the East in ships."[14]

It seems that John Denison Baldwin was onto something when he first suggested that the Phoenicians visited America. Indeed, the head depiction of the long-bearded Caucasian man carved on the ball court wall at Chichen Itza, if not of a Minoan ancestry, appears to be that of a Middle Eastern person.

While the Minoans and Phoenicians could be those behind the enigmatic maps of antiquity, when comparing the Minoan civilization to that of Atlantis, besides their DNA match, they also have similarities so striking that it leaves little doubt that these two cultures, separated by few millennia, were one and the same.

For instance, just as the Atlanteans before them, we know the Minoans were a mercantile society heavily involved in "global" trade. Both are known to have regularly traveled outside the Strait of Gibraltar, and both reportedly reached the American continent via the same route. Both the Atlanteans and the Minoans had a formidable Navy that helped them rule the Mediterranean and ensured that their coastal colonies remained safe. Both civilizations lived in unfortified cities, and both relied on their powerful Navy for protection. This further indicates that both were island civilizations as they had no fear of land invasion. Both seem to have practiced the same religion, with the bull being their primary idol.

Although, chronologically, both cultures were separated by nearly three millennia, both employed technologies ahead of their time and utilized similar architecture that was characterized by red, white, and black building material. Finally, and most importantly, "both" civilizations emerged from within the same region. In fact, a common ground that physically connects the two cultures, and ultimately brings the two civilizations closer together, is the small island of Santorini.

While Santorini is known historically as a Minoan settlement, the island's makeup of red, black, and white volcanic material physically matches Plato's description and location of where Atlantis's crown city once stood. More importantly, in addition to the island's natural composition, Santorini's physical shape (an island within an island setting) provides another striking resemblance. Does that mean Santorini itself could be Plato's lost island of Atlantis? Several skeptics argue with this suggestion. While Santorini may perfectly match Atlantis's capital city site, the island itself is too small to be the "grand island" Plato described. To these skeptics, neither Santorini nor the island of Crete (150 kilometers away), which some speculate was Atlantis's primary island, matches Plato's physical description. Suppose Santorini provides sound evidence that once was the location where Atlantis's capital city once stood, they ask, where then is the primary island, and how can Santorini fit into Plato's description?

So what do we know of Atlantis that could help in its discovery? According to Plato, he was repeating a story first revealed to Greek lawmaker Solon by Egyptian priests during one of his visits to Egypt. The Egyptians told Solon that at around 9,600 BC, Atlantis was a mighty naval empire that ruled many parts of southern Europe, North Africa, and the Middle East.

In 360 BC, in the dialogues of *Timaeus* and *Critias*, Plato described Atlantis in broader detail. In *Critias*, Plato depicted Atlantis as a large island with its northern portion consisting mostly of mountains that reached the shores. Just south of this mountainous region, he said that there was a great oblong valley that measured 3,000 stadia (roughly 555 square kilometers). Farther south, another smaller valley encircled by low-rise mountains measured 2,000 stadia (approximately 370 square kilometers). While this, according to Plato, made up the primary island of Atlantis, 50 stadia south of the primary island (precisely 9 kilometers away), there was another small circular island with a flooded center that contained another tiny island in it, about 5 stadia in diameter (about 0.92 kilometers). This setting of an island within an island, which undoubtedly resembles the locale of a sea volcano with a collapsed core, was the location where the crown city of Atlantis once stood. Plato said various bridges connected the tiny inner island to the cliffs of the outer island. A single narrow opening on this island's outer ring allowed ships to enter Atlantis's port in the island's flooded center. This detail reveals that the outer ring of land was surrounded by water, confirming that Atlantis's crown city was on a small island itself.

In his account, Plato further depicted Atlanteans as great architects and innovators involved in mass-scale agriculture. As he explained, irrigation to support the island's crops was produced by large water canals located in the primary island's central valley. In contrast, the mountains surrounding this central valley provided additional fresh water as well as timber for construction. Minerals were abundant on the island, including orichalcum, a particular copper type, which was the most valuable metal next to gold. In addition to domesticated animals, there were many wild animals on Atlantis's grand island, including numerous elephants. According to Plato, Atlantis was ultimately lost to the sea in a "single day and night" of misfortune.

Today, due to Santorini's striking resemblance to Plato's crown city of Atlantis, and the fact that the mysterious Minoan civilization appears to have many similarities with that of Atlantis, some historians are speculating that the Minoan civilization and Santorini itself must have been Plato's Atlantis. The concentric rings of earth and water around the center of the city, without a doubt, highly resemble the physical description of Santorini.

Another detail in Plato's description that further links Santorini to Atlantis was the presence of two natural springs, one of cold and one of hot water. Of course, as the origin of the hot water was geothermic, this further suggests that Atlantis must have been volcanic, just as Santorini is.

> The two springs, cold and hot, provided unlimited supply of water for appropriate purposes, remarkable for its agreeable quality and excellence.[15]

As previously mentioned, ongoing archaeological excavations on the island of Santorini and particularly at the city of Akrotiri, revealed that the 4,000-year-old city, fitted with sewers, had an elaborate supply system of hot and cold water.

Those not familiar with Santorini should know that the entire island is a massive volcano with a collapsed center. The enormous crater in the center of the island, about 12 kilometers wide at its widest part, is flooded with seawater and today serves as the island's idyllic port. There is a tiny uninhabited island in the center of this watery crater that allows Santorini to match Plato's description. Based on its striking resemblance, volcanic composition, and other similarities, is it possible to assume that Santorini may have been the location where

Atlantis's crown city once stood? Many skeptics disagree, saying the massive volcanic eruption of 1,600 BC must have hugely altered this island's shape. Several geological studies and other recent conclusions, though, point to quite the opposite. Surprisingly, it appears that the pre-eruption Santorini resembled Plato's city of Atlantis site even more.

In 1991, it was established by Druitt and Francaviglia that the ancient island of Santorini was made of concentric rings of land and sea even before the eruption. In fact, there is only one significant difference between the modern and prehistoric Santorini. It was determined that the caldera's outer ring that currently makes the primary island was nearly solid, with only a single opening to allow ship access into the island's watery center. Today, the post-eruption Santorini has three openings that enable ships to enter the watery caldera. Moreover, the small island in the center of the caldera, before the eruption of Santorini 3,600 years ago, was a much bigger island—large enough to match Plato's description and to hold the entire city center.

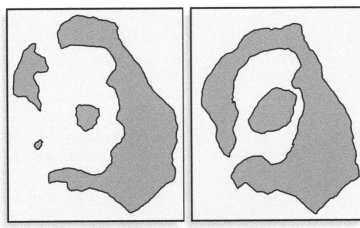

(Left) The island of Santorini, present day
(Right) Santorini before the eruption of 1,600 BC, according
to a 1991 study by Druitt and Francaviglia

It is worth mentioning that the volcanic eruption of Santorini, 3,600 years ago, was the second largest, if not the largest, in recorded history. The explosion was so intense that not only 60 cubic kilometers of magma and rock is estimated to have erupted from the volcano, but the event created several tsunamis of an unimaginable size that are said to have destroyed the Minoan civilization and its primary settlements around the Aegean Sea. The earthquakes and floods caused by the tsunamis were so damaging to the Minoans; many archaeologists agree that marked the end of the Minoan civilization as it was unable to recover afterward entirely.

The adverse natural phenomena that followed from this eruption were so notable in the entire region, including Egypt, that many scholars linked them to the book of Exodus's biblical events. Also, the visible watermarks reported by early explorers on the exterior limestone walls of the pyramids and eventually found in their interior could very well be the physical results of the enormous tsunami generated by Santorini's eruption.

When the Great Pyramid was first opened, it was reported that salt deposits' incrustations, up to 1 inch thick, were found inside the pyramid. Although some salt deposits were undoubtedly generated naturally, chemical analysis revealed that some of the salt from the pyramid's interior had a mineral content consistent with sea salt. While this discovery led to many bizarre theories in the past, when considering the topography of the Nile delta (a flat terrain barely a few feet above sea level), it is easy to see that a great tsunami like that of 1,600 BC could have quickly inundated the entire area, including the Giza Plateau situated at the beginning of the delta.

Once comparing this immense cataclysm to that of Atlantis, many people, especially those who believe that the Minoan Santorini was Atlantis, are convinced that the island's volcanic eruption was the catastrophe Plato was talking about.

> But afterwards there occurred violent earth-
> quakes and floods; and in a single day and night
> of misfortune all your warlike men in a body sank
> into the earth, and the island of Atlantis in like
> manner disappeared in the depths of the sea.[16]

The best we had on Plato's Atlantis until now was the island of Santorini, the Minoans, and the Santorini eruption of 1,600 BC. However, this was never a flawless hypothesis. A big problem with that theory was that Plato's given chronology of 9,600 BC had to be discarded. And yet there is another much bigger problem with that theory. While Santorini itself undeniably matches the very site where the crown city of Atlantis once stood (talking about the concentric rings of earth and water), a huge problem with that claim is that Santorini alone never matched Plato's full description. The primary island of Atlantis, the one Plato said was supposed to be 9 kilometers away from the circular island within an island, is missing from the setting of 1,600 BC. The lack of a perfectly matching site allowed for many critics in the past to raise doubts on Santorini and to continue to question the validity of Plato's story.

This inability to introduce a matching site out of Santorini alone more often becomes the juncture where many researchers, including supporters of the original Santorini hypothesis, begin to question the story's validity.

So is Atlantis real, or is it a myth? Contrary to the apparent difficulty in finding Atlantis, the truth is that Plato supplied us with enough information to locate the lost island and recognize it when found. We have the chronology of the event and a detailed physical description of the island. We also know of its volcanic composition, and we have all the details of the island's destruction, including a good portrayal of the aftermath. The information provided should be more than sufficient to help identify the island once found. Why, then, is there such great difficulty so far in finding it?

As previously suggested, in addition to other self-imposed difficulties, it seems that the biggest problem in locating Atlantis, by far, is that most people have been looking for it in the wrong period. As it seems, the only way to have found the primary island was to look for it in the right *chronology* rather than just in the right *topography*, as many people tend to do once they read the story. For example, while Plato made it clear that Atlantis's story took place around 9,600 BC, mainstream scientific conclusions and early account interpretations lead many people to look for Atlantis around the period of 1,600 BC and around the time when the Santorini volcano erupted.

This group of people ultimately realize that other than the island itself and the volcanic eruption that destroyed it—which are both convincing matches—nothing else seems to correspond to Plato's description. So as they arrive at a dead end, they either give up their search or continue to look for Atlantis elsewhere and sometimes in the most unusual places.

Of course, some put aside Plato's testimony altogether and, from the very beginning, follow their presumptions of what Atlantis once was. Often enough, these people are not only looking for Atlantis in the wrong time and continent, but most frequently, they are looking for an ultramodern civilization that never existed.

Alternatively, though, when one sets aside all personal interpretations and faithfully searches for Atlantis in the correct chronology (11,000 to 12,000 years ago) as if by a miracle, all the previously loose pieces of this great puzzle begin to fit.

First and foremost, the island of Atlantis, an island nearly the size of Crete, emerges from the sea 9 kilometers north of Santorini. This happens by lowering the Mediterranean Sea by 400 feet to correspond to the sea level during the tenth millennium BC when Plato said the Atlantis story took place.

Once the sea level is lowered, the Mediterranean looks like a whole different world. Many coastlines drastically change, and Greece and the island region around the Aegean Sea become nearly unrecognizable as several islands merge, including the Cyclades Islands, which were connected by a flat terrain, today called the Cyclades Plateau. This now-submerged plateau formed a large island, while the modern islands of Cyclades fashioned rows of mountains that emerged in all the right places. When comparing the submerged prehistoric island to Plato's Atlantis, it becomes clear that this must have been the place Plato was talking about. When still above water, the northern portion of this island was entirely comprised of mountains. There was an oblong valley just south of this mountainous region (roughly 555 square kilometers) and a second valley closer to the center of the island (approximately 370 square kilometers) encircled by low-rise mountains. Moreover, just as Plato depicted, this central valley was two-thirds the oblong valley's size. Not only does the primary island perfectly match Plato's physical description, but Santorini itself, a setting of an island within an island, falls precisely 9 kilometers away from the main island and just as Plato asserted.

Finally, we now have a tangible site where every physical aspect of the topography, the chronology, the volcanic geology, flora and fauna in that period (including the elephants), the island's destruction by a "Great Flood," remnants of a Neolithic civilization in the immediate area, and most importantly DNA evidence (see haplogroup X), all point to a perfect match.

An island comprising mostly of mountains in the northern portions and along the shore, and encompassing a great plain of an oblong shape in the south extending in one direction three thousand stadia (about 555 square kilometers; 345 square miles), but across the center island it was two thousand stadia (about 370 square kilometers; 230 square miles). Fifty stadia (9km; 6 miles) from the coast was a mountain that was low on all sides...broke it off all round about... the central island itself was five stades in diameter (about 0.92 km; 0.57 miles).[17]

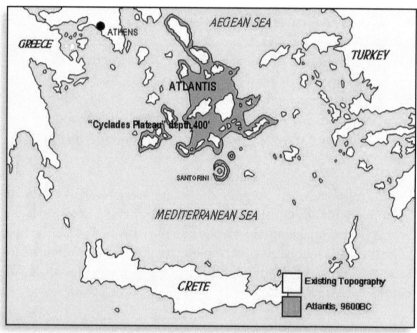

The island of Atlantis as described by Plato is revealed once the Mediterranean Sea level is lowered by 400 feet.

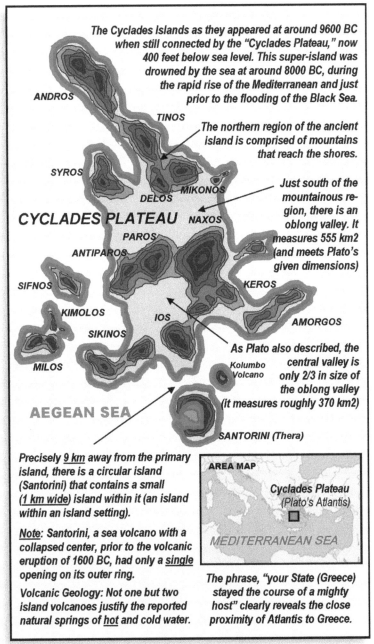

The Cyclades Islands as they appeared at around 9600 BC when still connected by the "Cyclades Plateau," now 400 feet below sea level. This super-island was drowned by the sea at around 8000 BC, during the rapid rise of the Mediterranean and just prior to the flooding of the Black Sea.

ANDROS

TINOS

The northern region of the ancient island is comprised of mountains that reach the shores.

SYROS

MIKONOS
DELOS

CYCLADES PLATEAU   NAXOS

Just south of the mountainous region, there is an oblong valley. It measures 555 km2 (and meets Plato's given dimensions)

PAROS
ANTIPAROS

SIFNOS

KEROS

KIMOLOS
IOS
SIKINOS

AMORGOS

MILOS

Kolumbo Volcano

As Plato also described, the central valley is only 2/3 in size of the oblong valley (it measures roughly 370 km2)

AEGEAN SEA

SANTORINI (Thera)

Precisely **9 km** away from the primary island, there is a circular island (Santorini) that contains a small (**1 km wide**) island within it (an island within an island setting).

<u>Note</u>: Santorini, a sea volcano with a collapsed center, prior to the volcanic eruption of 1600 BC, had only a <u>single</u> opening on its outer ring.

Volcanic Geology: Not one but two island volcanoes justify the reported natural springs of <u>hot</u> and cold water.

AREA MAP

Cyclades Plateau
(Plato's Atlantis)

MEDITERRANEAN SEA

The phrase, "your State (Greece) stayed the course of a mighty host" clearly reveals the close proximity of Atlantis to Greece.

The prehistoric super-island of the "Cyclades Plateau" (circa 9,600 BC). A perfect match to Plato's Atlantis.

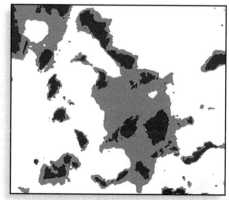

The primary island of Atlantis before the "Great Flood"

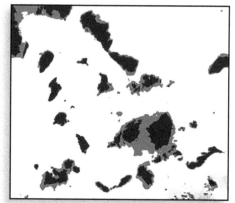

Atlantis after the initial inundation of the Cyclades Plateau

After the flood cycle ended, the mountaintops of Atlantis turned into small islets. Today, we know them as the Cyclades Islands.

Is there any chance, one may ask, that the matching site at hand may not be Plato's Atlantis? When considering how difficult it was in the past to find a perfectly matching site, one where all the required elements were present and in the perfect order, the odds of finding such a place can compare to correctly matching the lottery's winning numbers. In fact, when further considering that the lottery can be won regardless of which order the five winning numbers are drawn, finding a perfectly matching site where all the required elements must be in the right order may be more complicated than winning the lottery. Consequently, to dismiss a perfectly matching site, it may be as difficult as deliberating against the lottery's winning ticket. The only thing missing from this setting is a 10,000-year-old artifact, although finding one may be more complicated than it sounds.

While the Cyclades Islands are undeniably some of the most beautiful in the world, we must not forget that in the last 10,000 years, this region was carved into existence by one type of natural catastrophe after another. Horrendous earthquakes, unimaginable floods, tsunamis, and frequent volcanic eruptions all contributed to Atlantis's demise and these islands' formation. If Atlantean artifacts are not covered beneath several meters of soil or lying below 400 feet of water, they could have been blown to pieces during the 1,600 BC volcanic eruption of Santorini or during one of several other volcanic eruptions that occurred over the millennia. Dozens more, less powerful eruptions over the centuries, followed by enormous tsunamis, also took a toll on the surrounding islands. And if these conditions were not bad enough, a second volcano in the vicinity periodically caused its own set of disasters.

Although most people don't know this, another active volcano is 8 kilometers northeast of Santorini, with its top sitting just 60 feet beneath the waves. It is known as the Kolumbo volcano or *Koloumbos* in Greek. The last known eruption of Kolumbo occurred in AD 1650. It was a very violent event as it ejected pumice and ash as far as Turkey and produced pyroclastic flows that killed many people on Santorini at the time. A massive tsunami generated by the collapse of the volcano's cone also flooded several islands and caused severe damage up to 150 kilometers away.

Despite the apparent difficulties, however, we must remain hopeful. When looking for archaeological evidence, sometimes, with a little luck, anything is possible. Consider the 4,000-year-old city of Akrotiri that survived the unimaginable. Continuous excavations on Santorini and the surrounding islands, as well as at the bottom of the sea between the Cyclades Islands, may eventually reveal artifacts or ruins that will finally confirm a 10,000-year-old civilization in the area.

Skeptics, though, are never convinced. They argue that according to the story, Atlantis was swallowed by the sea and vanished, while obviously in this case, remnants of the island, along with Santorini, were left behind. Also, if not the Santorini eruption of 1,600 BC that seems to match Atlantis's demise perfectly, what other natural catastrophe after 9,600 BC, they ask, could come close to Plato's description of the end?

While moving forward, first and foremost, we must realize that Plato never mentioned Atlantis's exact end date. The 9,600 BC time frame given was when the story unfolded, and not necessarily when Atlantis was lost, as many automatically assume. Plato pointed out that Atlantis's end came at a *"later time"* and after a series of prolonged *"portentous earthquakes and floods."*

> But at a later time there occurred portentous earthquakes and floods, and one grievous day and night befell them,...And the island of Atlantis in like manner was swallowed up by the sea and vanished.[18]

The mere mention of earthquakes and floods by Plato in the plural form not only confirms that the island's destruction was more gradual, but this statement further corroborates that the periodic floods were most likely associated with the rise of the oceans as earlier indicated. Furthermore, the remark "one grievous day and night," more of a stock phrase among Greeks, does not necessarily imply that the island was lost within 24 hours but that the end event occurred at some unknown point in time.

Following Plato's description of the end, it reads as if for several decades, strong earthquakes and frequent floods (associated with the rise of the oceans) began to take a toll on the island. At some unknown point in time, before 8,000 BC and just before the flooding of the Black Sea, when the melting of the glaciers reached a climax and the ocean levels began to rise more aggressively, the sea level in the Mediterranean abruptly rose high enough to flood the valleys and lower elevations of Atlantis. This was the flood that essentially claimed the island. The flat terrain of the entire island became "impassable and impenetrable," and as Plato explained, "this was caused by the subsidence of the island." Of course, knowing nothing of the natural forces at play, Plato misinterpreted the sea's rise and called it the "gradual sinking" of the island.

> Wherefore also the ocean at that spot has now become impassable and unsearchable, being blocked up by the shoal of mud which the island created as it settled down.[19]

During this intense flood, the conditions must have been horrific as they presumably resembled those of New Orleans in 2005—or worse, those of the tsunami in Thailand in 2004 or Japan in 2011. This flood was so formidable that overnight it turned the Cyclades Plateau into a muddy sandbar or, as Plato best explained, into a "shoal of mud." One significant difference between the flood of Atlantis and those other natural disasters is that the floodwaters never receded from Atlantis. As the waters continued to rise, the island was forever surrendered to the sea.

This Great Flood and the devastation it brought to the island was what Plato was talking about. Not speaking in literal terms but dramatically, Plato said the island on that very day was "swallowed" (claimed) by the sea, and it "vanished." In another paragraph altogether, though, he further describes the particular region and explains that once the flood cycle finally ended, the island's mountaintops remained above water and formed small islands. Poetically once again, he compared these remaining islets to the "bones of the wasted body" of the "country" that once was there.

> The consequence is, that in comparison of what then was, there are remaining in small islets only the bones of the wasted body, as they may be called, all the richer and softer parts of the soil having fallen away, and the mere skeleton of the country being left.[20]

His description did not end there, however. He went even further and dramatically described the environmental transformation in the area between 9,000 BC and his own time—nearly seven millennia later. He explained that the heavily forested mountains, which once supplied timber of sufficient size to cover even the largest houses, became small islets that could barely provide "sustenance to bees." This is another vital piece of information where Plato perfectly depicts the total transformation of the region and explains how the once large, green islands of the Aegean, from ten millennia ago, ultimately became the small, dry islands we know today.

> But in former days, and in the primitive state of the country, what are now mountains were regarded as hills; and the plains they are now termed, of Phelleus were full of rich earth, and there was abundance of wood in the mountains. Of this last the traces still remain, for there are some of the mountains which now only afford sustenance to bees, whereas not long ago there

were still remaining roofs cut from the trees growing there, which were of a size sufficient to cover the largest houses; and there were many other high trees, bearing fruit, and abundance of food for cattle.[21]

There is little doubt that the flood that destroyed Atlantis and every coastal civilization around the planet simultaneously is the event that forever after would be referred to as the Great Flood.

In a scientific textbook on marine environments (2010), titled *Coastal and Marine Geospatial Technologies,* K. Gaki-Papanastasiou mentioned that the ancient Cycladic Island could have been the location where Plato's Atlantis once stood and further agreed that if Atlantis did exist, it was lost due to the rapidly rising seas.

> It is very possible that the famous ancient Atlantis was one of the flourishing city states on the large Cycladic Island (5,282 km^2) that was drowned following the rapid sea level rise between 18,000 and 7,000 years ago… The disappearance of Atlantis may not be owed to tectonic reasons (sudden submergence) but to eustatic ones (marine transgression). If we postulate that Atlantis was a city-state flourishing around 10,000–9,000 years Before Present, that it was located in the central Aegean Sea, and that the "old" Cycladic Island was diminishing quickly due to the rapid sea level rise, it becomes obvious that many coastal Neolithic settlements were drowned by the sea.[22]

Atlantis and other civilizations worldwide, like the submerged city off the coast of West India, or Atlit Yam off Israel's coast, all fell victim to the rising oceans. For the next 1,000 years, as the waters relentlessly continued to claim more and more dryland, all efforts to reignite any of these civilizations failed. This was a chaotic period where people remained scattered, and history ceased to exist.

At around 5,000 BC (once the oceans stabilized), we begin to see signs of human activity. A few centuries later, closer to 4,000 BC, we see an explosion of human civilizations that "mysteriously" seem to appear out of nowhere. The Sumerians emerged in Mesopotamia, the Harappan civilization developed in India, and in no time, the "Minoans" began to dominate over the entire Mediterranean. Practically overnight, these civilizations "became masters" in architecture and astronomy and possessed incredible skills that neither historians nor anthropologists can quite explain.

Unfortunately, due to the lack of tangible evidence, early historians failed to connect the dots and recognize that many of these cultures were around thousands of years earlier. We were unable to realize that the incredible megalithic structures and technological achievements of the fifth and fourth millennia BC were essentially part of an earlier "renaissance era" that immediately resumed once the oceans' rise ended. So when for the first time a post-Atlantean civilization was detected on Crete, due to the lack of clear identity, early archaeologists mistakenly renamed them Minoans after the mythical king of Crete, Minos.

While to this day it is not clear what Minoans called themselves, it appears that other ancient civilizations, especially the Egyptians, knew of their close relation to Atlantis. This revelation becomes more evident with their assertion to Solon that Atlantis was an old adversary of Greece. Strangely, by the time this information was revealed to Solon, Atlantis was already "lost in history." The post-Atlantean civilization of the Minoans also ended 800 years before that revelation. Although the Egyptians were fully aware that the Greeks were not around early enough to have met the so-called Atlanteans, they still named the Atlanteans an adversary of Greece. Why would they say that? Was that a mistake?

On the other hand, the Egyptians knew well that before their demise, the Minoans and the mainland Greeks were real enemies. Did the Egyptians make an identity mistake, or since they very well knew that the Minoans and the Atlanteans were one and the same, they took their knowledge for granted? Let us not ignore the fact that when the Minoan civilization was detected in 1905 and "nicknamed" by Sir Arthur Evans after the mythical King Minos, no one at the time, or in the decades that followed, ever found the real name of that civilization. Is it possible that Plato, as well as the Egyptians, already knew these people as Atlanteans? If so, if the Minoans ascended from the Atlanteans, as evidence shows, then it should not be a surprise seeing Plato, on the one hand, depicting the island of Atlantis while on the other hand describing aspects of their civilization from the Minoan era.

If anything, this knowledge has allowed Plato to introduce these people from their very early beginnings at around 9,600 BC, and through their ultimate demise by the mainland Greeks at about 1,500 BC. He depicted the Cyclades Plateau (or the island of Atlantis, if you will) before it was drowned by the rising seas. He described the Atlanteans' aggressive character toward their Mediterranean neighbors and others, and he correctly reported their incredible skills and their unwitting genetic contribution to history by crossing the Atlantic.

In regard to everyday details and their way of life, Plato chose to use aspects from a much later time in their history, the "Minoan" era. Was this because he did not know any better, or did he do that by choice? If Plato was crafting an ideological story around a real setting and a prehistoric civilization that managed to endure into the Bronze Age, one the Greeks ultimately defeated, then in order to successfully communicate some of his philosophical ideas (divine vs. human, ideal societies vs. corrupt), he needed details that his Greek audience would be more familiar with (Greek names, Greek gods, orichalcum, etc.). Could otherwise his ideological story appeal to his audience if they could not connect or relate to it?

Knowing that the Atlanteans and the Minoans were the same people, was Plato ever obligated to explain to his audience that he was
borrowing elements from two time periods? Although that was not
necessary, it would have been nice to know. Was such clarification of
paramount importance in conveying his moral account successfully?
Not really. By not being more transparent, did Plato lie in any way
about Atlantis, the Atlanteans, or the bulk of his story? He did not.
Was Plato's narrative based on real events, and should historians have
paid closer attention to Plato's testament rather than treating it as a
cautionary tale? Absolutely! Plato's claim that a Mediterranean race
reached North America around 11,000 years ago coincides with haplogroup X's arrival. He correctly stated that the migration took place
via the Atlantic, and the Atlanteans left behind traces of their presence (haplogroup X) on every island stop from Europe to America.
He correctly described the natural catastrophe and the Aegean's
transformation after the inundation of the prehistoric super-island.
Long before scientists conceded that the Minoans arose from an
older prehistoric civilization already in the area, it seems that Plato
already had linked the Minoans to the Atlanteans. Finally, he correctly stated that the Atlanteans (or Minoans if you prefer) fell victim
to mainland Greeks.

Indeed. Historically, we know that after the Santorini's eruption, the
Minoans lasted for another century or so. By then, the effects of that
disaster brought them to their knees and made them easy prey for
the Mycenean Greeks, who finally invaded Crete and helped put an
end to the Minoan era. The volcanic eruption of Santorini at 1,646
BC and the megatsunamis that followed marked the beginning of the
end for this post-Atlantean civilization. With their coastal cities and
villages on Crete and those on the surrounding islands destroyed,
and with Mycenaean Greeks now occupying their homeland, many
Minoans moved east and settled in Cyprus. Eventually, they moved
further east and settled on the shores of the Mediterranean between
Syria and Israel. According to historical accounts, it appears that the
mighty Minoans (or Atlanteans, if you will) did not "go quietly into
the night." While considering that they were, in effect, a "dead" civ-

ilization at that point in time, their influence in the area was enormous—to say the least.

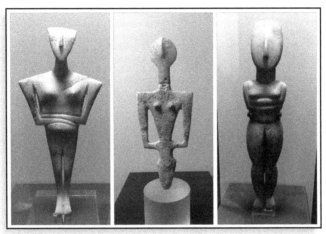

These prehistoric artifacts were found around the Cyclades Islands, and they predate both the Minoan and Greek civilization by a few thousand years. As DNA tests show that the Minoan civilization emerged from another proto-Minoan culture already around the Aegean, most likely, these are the remnants of the same post-Atlantean people who survived the inundation and later reorganized around the Cyclades Islands (originally the mountaintops of the super-island).

Cypro-Minoan scripts found in Cyprus and around the Middle East proved that the Linear A writing system, developed after the Minoan arrival on the island, had several shared characteristics with the Minoan Linear B system widely used on the island of Crete. Oddly enough, after studying the new Cypro-Minoan writing system and those who used it, mainstream historians decided to call these people Philistines. They furthermore credited the Linear A system to the "mysterious" and previously unknown Philistines, a literate culture of "sea people" that we are told originated from a region within the Aegean Sea and ultimately migrated to the eastern shores of the Mediterranean around 1,200 BC. Was this another case of mistaken identity? It seems that those Plato referred to as Atlanteans were first "identified" as the Minoans, then were labeled as "sea people," and finally were called the Philistines.

There should be no confusion among experts in this case. These mysterious sea people were primarily Minoan refugees mixed with other Aegean migrants who were uprooted not only by the volcanic eruption of Santorini itself but ultimately by the aftermath of that horrible and long-lasting disaster. Without considering the type of adverse conditions that immediately followed this particular volcanic eruption or how many years its effects lasted, a blast of that magnitude must have severely devastated the entire Aegean region and forced the inhabitants of that area to flee. If not right away, they undoubtedly fled in the years that followed.

Of course, there is another strong possibility. Santorini's eruption was not just an isolated incident during the end of the Bronze Age. It is highly speculated that the movement of the same tectonic plates that caused the earthquakes in the area and Santorini's eruption could have continued to produce a series of strong earthquakes in that region for another couple of centuries.

A recent study posted in *Stanford News Service* in 1997 titled "Don't Blame the Trojan Horse: Earthquakes Toppled Ancient Cities, Stanford Geophysicist Says" revealed that large earthquakes could be temporarily clustered. The study explained that when a tectonic plate ruptures in one place, it strains another part of the plate boundary and ultimately may cause its collapse after a short time. Until the entire plate boundary ruptures, a cascade of earthquakes can be produced. The intense activity period can be separated by long periods when the entire plate strains but does not entirely give. In that case, as the strain builds up, the earthquake cycle begins once again.

According to the study, it is believed that fifty or more cities around the eastern Mediterranean, between Greece and Israel, fell victim to prolonged earthquakes at the end of the Bronze Age, specifically just before 1,200 BC when the "sea people" first appeared. If so, it is not hard to envision that the societies affected, given their limited technology, immediately fell apart, thus creating a wave of refugees that traveled the region—by either land or water—and raided all other cities found intact for their survival. As the region in the Mediterranean primarily affected (either by the Santorini eruption or by the earthquakes that followed) was a Minoan territory, most of these refugees must have been of Minoan ancestry. Archaeological evidence has shown that the Santorini residents, along with their entire fleet, escaped the volcanic eruption. If so, where did they settle afterward? Crete, their primary colony, which was either destroyed by the tsunami or the earthquakes that followed, was eventually occupied by mainland Greeks. Is it possible that another society immediately welcomed the Minoan refugees in the area, or could they have turned into a culture of "sea people" who initially survived by preying on the entire region and others' wealth?

According to history, these Minoan refugees (or sea people, if you prefer) eventually settled along the Middle East's shores. Excavations at Ashkelon in Israel, a known Philistine city, proved that the writing inscribed on several clay pots was Cypro-Minoan. While most likely many of these pieces were imported from Cyprus or Crete by early settlers, a particular jar of local clay proved to be the work of a native post-Minoan culture there. However, there is more evidence to verify that the so-called sea people (or Philistines) were of Minoan ancestry. The ancient city of Gaza, yet another famous Philistine city, was initially called Minoah, a name clearly founded by Cretans.

The influence of the Minoans on the island of Cyprus was also quite significant. For starters, the language transformation on the island to Linear A was so widespread that it led some historians to theorize that the enigmatic Philistines may have originated there. Despite the prevailing scientific confusion, though, it is also worth to mention that Cyprus is the only country in the world that annually still holds a weeklong celebration in remembrance of the Great Flood. Although its Christian population links this popular festival to the biblical flood, is it also possible that it essentially commemorates an event that over the millennia was kept alive by the so-called sea people or, better yet, the post-Atlantean Minoans?

To better understand how the climatic and ecological changes (and ultimately the rise of the sea) affected coastal civilizations in the Mediterranean, one must follow the work of Dr. Francois Doumenge (director of the Oceanographic Institute of Monaco and secretary-general of the International Commission for the Scientific Exploration of the Mediterranean Sea, Monaco).

In 1996, Dr. Doumenge gave a presentation at the United Nations University Headquarters. Although his presentation had nothing to do with archaeology or anthropology directly, Dr. Doumenge presented a long-term historical look of the Mediterranean and the series of environmental crises that had affected it over the millennia. To a certain extent, he confirmed past theories that during the Messinian period, the Strait of Gibraltar had remained closed for 100,000 to 200,000 years, during which time the Mediterranean had evaporated entirely. This, he explained, happened several times between 5 and 6 million years ago. Consequently, the Mediterranean's dry basin retained giant salt deposits with a total volume exceeding 1.5 million square kilometers. The total water evaporation between 5 and 6 million years ago and its continuous evaporation and refill of seawater from the Atlantic or the Red Sea also explain the higher salinity currently found in the Mediterranean.

Dr. Doumenge also revealed that the Mediterranean went through another crisis during the last Ice Age beginning 18,000 years ago. He explained that not only had the last Ice Age caused severe effects on the Mediterranean's ecosystem, but the 400-foot lower sea level had exposed hundreds of thousands of square miles of land.

The Adriatic Sea was mostly dryland, the Aegean Sea was about 40% smaller, and the enlarged Sicilian and African coast, at modern-day Tunisia, nearly merged. The much smaller Black Sea, a freshwater lake at that time, was heavily draining into the Mediterranean with its water flowing southward along the coast of modern-day Turkey to Africa's northern coast.

During the last Ice Age, the combined effects were so profound that the Mediterranean Basin was divided into three separate ecosystems. The far eastern portion of the Mediterranean, which was practically cut off by the stream of fresh water that flowed down from the Black Sea, remained warmer, and the region around Egypt and Cyprus was more like a semitropical setting. This early semitropical climate in the prehistoric Middle East also explains the existence of the Fertile Crescent. A fertile territory that extended from the Nile valley followed the eastern Mediterranean coast to southeastern Turkey and then turned southward toward the Mesopotamia region and the shores of the Persian Gulf. This area, which ultimately became the cradle of civilization as we know it, was also the home of eight Neolithic originator crops important to early agriculture and four of the five most important species of domesticated animals (cows, goats, pigs, and sheep).

The central Mediterranean, in contrast, maintained its current temperature and characteristics. The Western Basin, connected and continuously refilled via the Strait of Gibraltar, retained much colder temperatures like those of the North Sea. This also explains the large population of blue whales in the western part of the Mediterranean, still present to this day.

While reviewing Dr. Doumenge's study from 1996, as well as the latest research reported in *Science News* in 2010, we realize that the planet went through a massive cataclysm that started around 13,000 BC, intensified between 9,000 BC and 8,000 BC, and finally began to stabilize between 7,000 BC and 5,000 BC. During this period, not only did the seas rise by 400 feet or more, but the rising waters seem to have literally swallowed all physical evidence that could suggest the existence of another advanced civilization during our prehistory.

Is it possible, however, that all traces of prehistoric civilizations are entirely lost? Although archaeological sites like that of Gobekli Tepe help validate their existence, unfortunately, the burden of proof rests with sunken cities, like those off the west coast of India and that of Atlantis. Should we assume then that the evidence of all past civilizations lay at the bottom of the sea, or is it possible somehow that more artifacts in higher elevations may have survived and await our discovery?

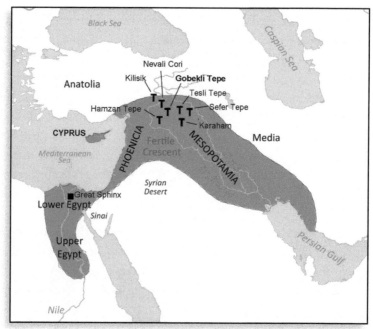

The Fertile Crescent (8,000 BC) was a fertile territory that extended from the Nile valley in Egypt. It followed the coast of eastern Mediterranean to southwestern Turkey and then turned down southward toward the Mesopotamia region and the shores of the Persian Gulf. Gobekli Tepe and other prehistoric sites with T-shape pillars are located within the northern portion of the crescent, between Euphrates and Tigris Rivers.

Fortunately, science never ceases to surprise us. On October 23, 1991, an amazing article in the *Los Angeles Times* caught many people's attention. The article was titled "Sphinx's New Riddle: Is It

Older Than Experts Say? Archeologists, Geologists Cite Study of Weathering Patterns, but Egyptologists Say Findings Can't Be Right."

As the title of the article insinuates, after extensive geological research on the Giza Plateau and the Great Sphinx at that time, the evidence pointed to the possibility that the Sphinx may be at least twice as old as the pyramids and could conservatively date as far back as 7,000 BC, if not older.

As expected, such an announcement caused a firestorm of controversy and a fierce argument among mainstream archaeologists since such a conclusion contradicted everything the mainstream academia "knew" about ancient Egypt.

When geologists presented their results at the Geological Society of America, they mentioned that the weather patterns on the monument convinced them that they were from another period much older than previously estimated. Until then, Egyptologists and mainstream archaeologists thought the Pharaoh Khafre had built the Sphinx at around 2,500 BC. After a series of unprecedented studies at the Giza site, though, evidence suggested that the monument had already been there for thousands of years before Khafre.

More specifically, the research team noticed that the Sphinx was carved into a limestone bedrock and essentially sits inside a ditch. The walls of this ditch offered the researchers the first tantalizing clues. They were heavily weathered by water, suggesting that the ditch was dug much earlier than 3,000 BC, when rainfall in the area was much heavier than it has been in the last few thousand years. Of course, as mentioned earlier, according to Dr. Doumenge, the last time rainfall in this area was heavy would have been around 8,000 BC, during the rise of the Mediterranean and before the flooding of the Black Sea.

Joining geologist Robert M. Schoch of Boston University in the research were Thomas L. Dobecki, a Houston geophysicist, and John Anthony West, an Egyptologist of New York.

The scientific team showed that the limestone bed surrounding the monument, part of which was exposed when the Sphinx was first carved, has weathered far longer than had been previously thought. Also, significant erosion differences between the Sphinx and other structures of unmistakable origin further indicated that the Sphinx was a much older structure.

The team also conducted the first seismic tests ever allowed at the site, which essentially reveal the age of a structure by measuring how sound waves move through rock. As weathering creates pores in rocks, the speed at which the waves travel can tell scientists about the rock's porosity, and the sound waves can measure how much of a structure has weathered. In turn, that tells them how long it has been exposed to the elements.

Needless to say, and as expected, Egyptologists continue to maintain that the Great Sphinx must have been the creation of Khafre, not only because it is contained within the same tomb complex but also, as they indicate, the face of the Sphinx also resembles Khafre. Interestingly, though, the same type of tests on the Sphinx face noted that the head is as old as its body, making it much older than the rest of the monuments. Ultimately, Mr. Schoch and his team concluded that when Khafre began construction on this site, not only could he have refurbished the monument, but he also could have altered the face.

If Mr. Schoch and his team are correct in their assessment, a few questions remain to be answered. Who constructed the Great Sphinx nearly 10,000 years ago, and why? Is it possible that the rise of the Egyptian civilization around the third millennium BC was not a new development but a legacy that continued over a much older culture in the area? Even more importantly, does the conclusion of another prehistoric civilization erecting this great structure further validate all other rumors surrounding this monument?

More accurately, it has been claimed that there are cavities under the Sphinx, including one that holds the Hall of Records. For those not familiar with this story, the Hall of Records is believed to be a small chamber beneath the Sphinx that housed Atlantis's history. It is also how, reportedly, Egyptian priests initially became aware of the lost civilization.

Surprisingly enough, the belief that there are cavities below the monument, as well as a tomb belonging to King Harmais, is not a recent claim. This was first suggested by Pliny the Elder (23 AD–79 AD), a renowned Roman author and military commander, which he wrote:

> The other three pyramids, the fame of which has reached every part of the world, are of course visible to travelers approaching by river from any direction. They stand on a rocky hill in the desert on the African side of the river between the city of Memphis and what, as we have already explained, is known as the Delta, at a point less than 4 miles from the Nile, and 7 ½ miles from Memphis. Close by is a village called Busiris, where there are people who are used to climbing these pyramids.
>
> In front of them is the Sphinx, which deserves to be described even more than they, and yet the Egyptians have passed it over in silence. The inhabitants of the region regard it as a deity. They are of the opinion that a King Harmais is buried inside it and try to make out that it was brought to the spot: it is in fact carefully fashioned from the native rock. The face of the monstrous creature is painted with ruddle as a sign of reverence. The circumference of the head when measured across the forehead amounts to 102 feet, the length is 243 feet, and the height from the paunch to the top of the asp on its head is 61 ½ feet.[23]

While modern-day archaeologists categorically deny the existence of such a chamber, ground-penetrating radar implies that indeed, there are unexplained cavities below this monument. If so, was Pliny the Elder correct? As other researchers previously asserted, is it possible to accept that at around 10,500 BC, Atlanteans sealed the hall away with records of their accumulated knowledge, just as the Hebrews did with the Dead Sea Scrolls 8,000 years later?

Many mainstream Egyptologists disagree. In fact, not only do they deny such claims, but surprisingly, they also dismiss Mr. Schoch's research. According to them, "the people of that region would not have had the technology, the governing institutions, or even the will to build such a structure thousands of years before Khafre's reign." Why do they dismiss scientific research, though, and insist on their previous conclusions? Their assessment that the Great Sphinx is a much older structure was not reached without the scientific data to support it. Selectively ignoring the scientific results and the notion of "what we do not know or do not understand simply does not exist" is far from scientific. Taking such a position against the evidence, not to mention ancient testimony, nearly takes us back to a time when we insisted that the Earth was flat.

Incidentally, though, just when more critics started to remind us that no one so early in time could have constructed the monument of the Sphinx, to everyone's amazement, another remarkable discovery in the Mediterranean region proved once again that our ancestors 12,000 years ago were more advanced and capable than we are willing to give them credit for. Without a doubt, this latest finding not only reinforces Mr. Schoch's claim that the Sphinx could have been created 10,000 years ago, but it further confirms Plato's testimony of another advanced civilization in the area during our prehistory.

On February 19, 2010, *Newsweek* published an article titled "History in the Remaking: A Temple Complex in Turkey That Predates Even the Pyramids Is Rewriting the Human Evolution."

Gobekli Tepe, currently the world's oldest archaeological site, is estimated to have been erected 12,000 years ago, if not earlier. It is a massive site that features twenty large round structures, each up to 30 meters (100 feet) in diameter. Each round structure features massive, T-shaped pillars (some up to 6.9 meters or 22 feet in height), which at one point held a roof system overhead. Carvings of animals on these T-shaped pillars include foxes, lions, hyenas, cranes, ducks, scorpions, and snakes—among others.

Although not a great deal is known of this incredible archaeological site that predates the pyramids by at least 7,000 years, Gobekli Tepe further validates previous claims that prehistoric humans were more organized and advanced than historians and anthropologists were previously willing to accept.

Contrary to the mounting evidence that points toward such a conclusion, some skeptics still argue that Gobekli Tepe refutes the idea of an organized society at the time for its structures, according to them, were constructed without the infrastructure of a known civilization. Is it possible, then, that two dozen or more monumental assemblies on this site that imply certain complexity and organization that rivals those of ancient Sumer were constructed by a horde of hunters and gatherers in their spare time, or does Gobekli Tepe itself makes a case for such early human organization?

We must also not ignore the possibility that this megasite, although initially labeled by its founders as a place of worship, could have been an early human settlement instead. Evidence of daily activities, such as flint knapping and food preparation, suggests that Gobekli Tepe could have been partially a residential site with a small population. In a study published in *Current Anthropology* in 2011, archaeologist Ted Banning of the University of Toronto argued that some of the large buildings, especially those with the decorative pillars, could have been large communal houses "similar in some ways to the large plank houses of the northwest coast of North America with their impressive house posts and totem poles." If so, Banning said, "they would likely have housed quite large households, an extremely early example of what the French anthropologist, Claude Lévi-Strauss, called 'house societies.' Such societies often use house structures for competitive display, locations for rituals, and explicit symbols of social units."

Additional prehistoric settlements in the region carrying circular structures like that of Khirokitia in Cyprus or the city of Jericho in Palestine, and others, not only suggest that its builders could have occupied Gobekli Tepe, but this megasite reinforces the suggestion of an advanced prehistoric civilization in the region.

Is it possible that Gobekli Tepe and the Great Sphinx are remnants of the same advanced civilization Plato was talking about, one that aggressively was advancing eastward against its neighbors?

> ...a mighty host, which,...was insolently advancing
> to attack the whole of Europe, and Asia to boot.

If so, is it also possible to further assume that the oppressed, after the cataclysm and at the first opportunity, buried the outpost of Gobekli Tepe, thus eliminating the possibility for the trespassers ever reestablishing control over that area? According to the chief archaeologist at Gobekli Tepe, Klaus Schmidt, the site was not only abandoned abruptly around 8,000 BC, but it was deliberately buried all at once. This is how archaeologists explained most of the structures on this site remained intact.

This would not be the first time that oppressed people took advantage of a natural disaster to attack their oppressors. When a massive earthquake hit Sparta in 464 BC claiming the lives of twenty thousand Spartans, during the chaos that followed, the Helots (an oppressed population to Spartans) revolted against Sparta with hope to free themselves. Indeed, as Spartans were unable to defeat them, they reached an agreement that allowed Helots to leave Peloponnese (the place Sparta had settled in) and never return.

What happened to the Atlantean oppressors, though? Where did they go after they lost control of the region? Did they disappear?

Of course not. Just like the post-Atlantean Minoans, after the volcanic eruption of Santorini they scattered eastward, is it possible that the last Great Flood forced remnants of that once advanced culture deeper into the Mesopotamian region, where they ultimately helped the local population establish yet another great civilization, like that of ancient Sumer? Is it possible that refugees of this Mediterranean culture, which slowly dissented upon the Mesopotamian region between 8,000 and 7,000 BC, brought with them the story of the "Great Flood" and, along with it, some of their technological skills, including agriculture and astronomy? If not, who then were the "mysterious" Proto-Euphratean people, as archaeologists call them today, who descended to Mesopotamia from a region "unknown" and laid the foundation for the Sumerian civilization to build upon?

From historical movements of haplogroup X, we know that this eastern Mediterranean culture not only moved east toward the Mesopotamia region, but they kept on moving all the way to southern Russia and the Altai Republic region, the furthest point eastward found to have traces of haplogroup X.

While the majority moved toward modern-day Turkey and Greece, others moved further west either by foot or by boat. Those by boat must have followed the same island route westward (England, Orkney Islands, Faroe Islands, Iceland) until once again, they ended up in North America, where they left more of their genetic fingerprint behind. This, perhaps, not only explains why the second-highest concentration of haplogroup X away from the Mediterranean exists around Newfoundland and the Great Lakes, but this final wave west also explains the fact that some scientists now believe that there was not one but two distinct transatlantic migrations of haplogroup X to North America during our prehistory.

Why, though? Why the mass exodus from the Middle East after the oceans had already stabilized? Let us not ignore the fact that after the last Ice Age ended, the eastern Mediterranean, the Middle East, and the Fertile Crescent began to transform as well. Century by century, the temperatures in that region began to rise, and ultimately, the once semitropical territory turned into the dry region we all know today. Even those who initially fled inland to escape the inundation eventually had to leave once again in search of fertile territories to grow crops and raise animals.

Knowing this, it came not as a big surprise to hear that recent DNA evidence revealed that those who built Stonehenge in southern England were a culture from the eastern Mediterranean, who descended upon the region thousands of years earlier. In other words, these Middle Easterners could have very well been refugees of the same post-Atlantean culture that dispersed after the rise of the oceans and kept on moving westward, looking for a new homeland and favorable conditions to reestablish themselves. After all, the study pointed out that some of these Mediterranean people arrived in England with boats via island hopping. If so, is it possible then to assume that Stonehenge, just like Gobekli Tepe, was another circular monumental identity "marker" erected by the same Mediterranean people, another exhibit perhaps that bounded their presence in their newly found "homeland"? Just like other great monuments, like the pyramids of Egypt and those of Mesopotamia and Central America, not only those structures represented ceremonial assemblies, but to outsiders, these were undeniable symbols of strength and ability.

Truly, aside their ultimate purpose or functionality, the presence of megalithic structures was always of great importance for most civilizations around the world. From Paleolithic to Neolithic times, all the way to the Bronze Age and beyond, there are thousands of megalithic projects and structures around the world that simply symbolize the power of those who erected them.

An article posted by BBC News on April 16, 2019, noted,

Stonehenge: DNA reveals origin of builders.

Researchers compared DNA extracted from Neolithic human remains found across with that of people alive at the same time in Europe.

98

The Neolithic inhabitants were descended from populations originating in Anatolia (modern Turkey) that moved to Iberia before heading north. They reached Britain in about 4,000 BC. (Details have been published in the journal Nature Ecology & Evolution.)

The migration to Britain was just one part of a general, massive expansion of people out of Anatolia in 6,000 BC that introduced farming to Europe. Before that, Europe was populated by small, travelling groups which hunted animals and gathered wild plants and shellfish.

DNA reveals that Neolithic Britons were largely descended from groups who took the Mediterranean route, either hugging the coast or hopping from island-to-island on boats.[24]

In light of that, knowing now that Stonehenge was erected by a group of migrating Middle Easterners who began arriving in England by boats at around 4,000 BC, is it possible perhaps to further assume that a dozen more, not-so-profound megalithic sites with circular stone arrangements around England, Ireland, Scotland, and Orkney Islands could all possibly be additional territorial or identification markers progressively erected by the same people as they claimed additional territories? After all, when comparing megalithic stone sites like the Druid's Circle, Swinside Stone Circle, Castlerigg, Rollright Stones, Drombeg Stone Circle, Carrigagulla Stone Circle, Callanish Stones, and Ring of Brodgar, among several other sites, not only these circles appear to have been erected in the same fashion by the same culture, but incidentally, all have been raised during the third millennium BC.

Stonehenge, Salisbury, England (c. 3,000 BC)

(Left) Castlerigg Stone Circle, North West England
(Right) Swinside Stone Circle, near Millom, England
(Bottom) Druid's Circle, Penmaenmawr, England

While some of these sites seem to bear astronomical alignments, thus leading some experts to believe the stone circles' sole purpose was to serve as star observatories, others, like Kenneth Brophy of the University of Glasgow in Scotland, emphasize that there is nothing we can see in prehistoric people that suggests they had this highly mathematical view of the world. Indeed, astronomy alone cannot explain why there was ever a need to raise such colossal projects like Stonehenge for the sake of following the Moon and the Sun. For that purpose alone, just an ordinary assembly should have sufficed.

Of course, others believe that stone circles were places where social rituals could have taken place to honor the dead. While, indeed, there is evidence of burials and cremations at some of these sites, most notably at Stonehenge, erecting a monumental structure like Stonehenge with the sole intent of using it as a cemetery or for performing rituals still defies logic.

It is important to remember that these megalithic projects, which seem to appear out of nowhere in England, Ireland, Scotland, and other places around the world, all most likely can be attributed to the same group of Middle Easterners who during the third millennium BC descended upon these lands in search of a new home. Erecting stone circles and engraving identification symbols were most likely how these people marked their newly claimed territories and conveyed their presence.

After all, we must not ignore that land claim by stone staking or stone piling was a common practice from antiquity to modern times. During the United States's colonial period, American men continued to claim a piece of land for themselves by staking it. Later on, in modern times, mining claims in the United States similarly marked the claim boundaries, either with wooden posts, capped steel posts, or stone cairns 3 feet tall.

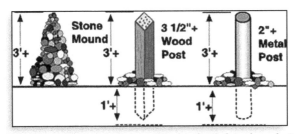

Federal law in the United States specifies that land claim boundaries must be distinctly and marked to be readily identifiable. Most state laws require conspicuous and substantial monuments for all types of claims and sites. The above are generalized examples of conspicuous and substantial monuments.

If the stone circles were territorial markers, though, or ancient calendar arrangements that foresaw the coming of the seasons (allowing people to know when to plant or harvest their crops), once again, why their enormous size? The decision to refabricate a structure that could have otherwise functioned at a smaller scale, and transform it into something colossal, clearly points to the likelihood that there was another purpose behind that need. What if these stone circles were not only ritual assemblies, but they meant to signify the status and ability of those who erected them, as Kenneth Brophy also suggested? "We have to understand these people through power structures in society, rather than emphasizing arcane mathematical measurements."

Moreover, while to onlookers the size of these monuments undoubtedly meant to signify the sheer power of those who raised them, we must not ignore the possibility that these megalithic assemblies, just as the carved concentric rings on standing stone piles, could have also served as symbols of identity as they memorialized these people's place of origin.

Just as Christians, Muslims, Jews, and other cultures in the last 2,000 years have been identifying themselves with their own religious signs, stone circles and markings depicting concentric rings meant not only to commemorate these people's place of origin (a circular island featuring concentric rings of earth and water), but in essence, these symbols could also have been used for cultural identification when far from home. Stone circles and markings with concentric rings must have been their "calling card" or trademark, if you will.

(Left) A carving with concentric rings found on a standing stone in southern Spain in 2018 led some researchers to jump into the wrong conclusions prematurely. As they may not have been aware that few more nearly identical carvings exist in England and in other places, they thought their find was unique and assumed that Plato's Atlantis could be in the immediate area. (Right) A carving with concentric rings found on a standing stone at the Long Meg Stone Circle in England (circa 3,000 BC) is nearly identical with the one found in Spain. Both images feature a single entrance leading to the center of the circle. One denotes the opening with arrows and the other with a straight line.

Likewise, before the cross became the official symbol of Christianity, during the first centuries after Christ, while Christianity was expanding around the Mediterranean, but the Romans persecuted the faithful, Christians widely used the fish symbol to denote meeting places and places of worship, mark tombs in catacombs, and ultimately to distinguish friends from foes. Seeing the fish, believers knew they were in good company.

As for the stone circles, it is of particular interest that in Greek, the name *Cyclades* means "a cycle or circular formation." Indeed, after the inundation of the super-island, the mountaintops surrounding the oblong valley turned into a circle of islands. It is also important to mention that the Cyclades's name is not modern, but it dates back to antiquity. Is there any significance in that?

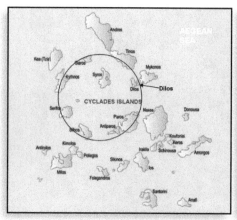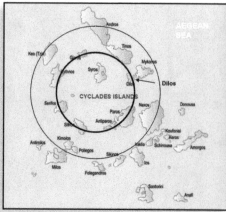

The Cyclades Islands (once mountaintops of the prehistoric island of Atlantis) form a "circle" in the Aegean Sea after the inundation.

Archaeologists today will say that ancient Greeks gave the Cyclades Islands their name because they form a rough circle around the island of Delos, Artemis's and Apollo's birthplace. The problem with that theory, however, is that the island of Delos is not even close to the circle's center but is part of the circle itself. Is it possible then that archaeologists are mistaken in their assumption? If the Cyclades's name dates back to antiquity, isn't it more probable that the original inhabitants of the super-island, and not the Greeks, are those behind the particular name? Besides, the Greeks themselves were also a by-product of this prehistoric pre-Cycladic civilization.

More precisely, the Myceneans and the Minoans, as we know them today, both ascended from this same group of people who managed to escape the inundation a few millennia earlier. Those who migrated to Crete reestablished themselves as the Minoan civilization during the third millennium BC, while those who moved to neighboring Greece reemerged during the second millennium BC as the Mycenaeans. A recent study of ancient DNA certainly confirmed that the Minoans and Mycenaeans were genetically extremely similar and that the modern Greeks ultimately ascended from these "two" populations. The study also pointed out that the ancestors of the Minoans and Mycenaeans were a culture of Neolithic farmers, another detail that further validates Plato's claim that those he called Atlanteans were involved in mass-scale agriculture.

Even though many historians today support the opinion that over time the Minoans greatly influenced the Myceneans, the truth is they fail to recognize that both of these civilizations go back and connect to the same pre-Cycladic culture who survived the inundation. What historians perceive to be influences are truly heritable connections between the "two cultures." Indeed, both civilizations use similar architecture, both bury their dead in circular structures called "tholoi," both share similar art, and both are known to be merchant societies.

Knowing this, knowing that these people were aware of their past and they were able to carry forward some of their earliest trades and traditions, is it possible to accept that the name Cyclades was also a name given to this cluster of islands by either one of these two post-Cycladic groups, which the Greeks later embraced? Of course, it is possible. Is it also conceivable to further assume that the stone circle formations erected by these people in foreign lands, following the Great Flood and through the third millennium BC, were in remembrance of their homeland and the circle of islands left behind? If so, like the stone circles could have commemorated the super-island's transformation, the carvings of concentric rings symbolized the site where Atlantis's crown city once stood.

Just like persecuted Christians did, as the Atlanteans continued to migrate further and further away from their homeland and in the process claimed more lands, they also continued to erect stone circles or carve markings with concentric rings to denote their presence.

The fact that identical carvings on standing stones exist in different countries and locations, with heavy traces of haplogroup X, further supports the notion that the same group of people created the circle stone formations and the carvings on stone piles. After all, these carvings and circles appear to be in countries and places where haplogroup X (or better yet Plato's Atlanteans) would have sailed by or settled down while traveling from the Mediterranean to the New World in search of a new home.

Indeed, several sites feature carved symbols of concentric rings and megalithic circle formations in England, Ireland, Scotland, and around the Mediterranean. Not only do we see these on land, but as it appears, some ended up underwater, either lost to the rising seas along with the Cyclades Plateau or in the years to follow.

Weetwood Moor, northeast England. Just like the carving at the Long Meg (northwest England) and that of southern Spain, this is another carving circa 3,000 BC on a stone that depicts the same structure of concentric rings with a single channel/entrance leading to its center.

A similar rock carving in Carshenna, Switzerland

A rock carving at the La Bessa site in Italy referred to as a "cup and rings" is another carving as all others found around Europe.

The monument at Rujm el-Hiri, Golan Heights, is dated at 3,000 BC. The concentric rings of this monument are made of forty-two thousand stacked stones. It also has an opening to its left side as in the case of the carvings in Spain and England.

Atlit Yam, off the coast of Atlit in Israel, is one such Neolithic settlement lost to the rising seas.

In 1984, marine archaeologist Ehud Galili first spotted its ancient ruins while surveying the area for shipwrecks. Instead, remains of rectangular houses and hearth places were found. Carbon dating found the site to be roughly 8,300 years old, a period that coincides with the end of the Mediterranean's flood cycle.

What is most notable about this 40,000-square-meter (10-acre) site is that the settlement is defined by a megalithic stone circle, just like the circles commonly seen in various places in Europe and England. This discovery not only helps identify the occupants of Atlit Yam, but it further corroborates a previous conclusion that the practice of erecting circles must have started after the inundation, and as more evidence shows, the tradition ended with their final migration west during the third millennium BC, just before the beginning of our recorded history. By then, the era of human migration ended, and the era of protecting established territories began.

As for Atlit Yam, although the site was eventually lost to the rising seas, ironically, a closer examination revealed that the rising sea was not the cause behind the site's abandonment. Piles of fish ready for trade or storage found on the site led scientists to conclude that the village was abandoned rather abruptly.

An Italian study led by Maria Pareschi of the Italian National Institute of Geophysics and Volcanology in Pisa showed that a volcanic collapse of the eastern flank of Mount Etna, roughly 8,500 years ago, was likely the cause of that. The study showed that the landslide from the collapsed volcano into the sea generated a gigantic tsunami 40 meters (130 feet) in height, which engulfed several coastal Neolithic sites in the eastern Mediterranean within hours, including Atlit Yam. The tsunami not only destroyed much of the settlement upon impact, but it was later determined that it contaminated the freshwater wells around the settlement, forcing people to abandon the site permanently.

The Etna disaster, which must have flooded several other coastal settlements, validates an earlier conclusion that the region around the eastern Mediterranean and the Aegean islands were ultimately defined by one natural disaster after another. Plato's mention of earthquakes and floods in the plural form not only implied that the destruction of Atlantis was gradual but further suggested that the whole eastern Mediterranean went through a significant transformation after the sea inundated the island of Atlantis.

Once the rising seas flooded the Cyclades Plateau and the super-island inhabitants realized that the sea was rising, not retreating, many began to abandon the island's higher elevations and began to flee inland, looking for new coastlines to reestablish themselves. Unfortunately, as they had no idea that the oceans would keep on rising for another thousand years, they continued rebuilding while the rising seas claimed more and more coastal settlements.

An article published by *Plos One* on December 18, 2019, with the title "A submerged 7,000-year-old village and seawall demonstrate earliest known coastal defense against sea-level rise," reported that underwater archaeological investigations off the Carmel Coast of Israel (near Atlit Yam) found fifteen additional submerged Neolithic settlements at various depths along the coast. One of those submerged settlements, Tel Hreiz, featured a seawall meant to protect the site from sea-level rise. This discovery proves a couple of earlier conclusions. At first, the seawall's existence demonstrates that Neolithic people were aware of the rising seas. The fact that fifteen more settlements were found submerged at various depths alongside the Carmel Coast also reveals that they had no idea how long this phenomenon will last, so every time they retreated inland to escape the inundation, they remained near ancient coastlines. This discovery finally confirms that most evidence of early human development, at least until the oceans stabilized, are to be found at various depths below sea level.

A submerged 7000-year-old village and seawall demonstrate earliest known coastal defence against sea-level rise.

We report the results of underwater archaeological investigations at the submerged Neolithic

settlement of Tel Hreiz (7500–7000 BP), off the
Carmel coast of Israel. The underwater archaeological site has yielded well-preserved architectural, artefactual, faunal and human remains.
We examine and discuss the notable recent discovery of a linear, boulder-built feature >100m
long, located seaward of the settlement. Based
on archaeological context, mode of construction and radiometric dating, we demonstrate
the feature was contemporary with the inundated Neolithic settlement and conclude that it
served as a seawall, built to protect the village
against Mediterranean Sea-level rise. The seawall is unique for the period and is the oldest
known coastal defence worldwide. Its length, use
of large non-local boulders and specific arrange-
ment in the landscape reflect the extensive effort
invested by the Neolithic villagers in its concep-
tion, organisation and construction. However,
this distinct social action and display of resilience
proved a temporary solution and ultimately the
village was inundated and abandoned...

A total of fifteen Neolithic settlements that were
inundated by post-glacial sea-level rise have been
discovered along a 20km off the Carmel coast
of northern Israel. Before inundation, the sites
were rapidly covered by a layer of sand which
contributed to their preservation.

Archaeological analyses of these submerged settlements have demonstrated that there is a correlation between depth and site age. The older sites
are found deeper and farther offshore than the
younger sites, located closer to the modern-day
shore. This also represents a direct correlation

between sea-level rise and the abandonment of coastal settlements and their translocation eastward. The earliest recorded submerged site, Atlit-Yam, is located 200–400m offshore, at a depth of -8 to -12m, and represents a permanent, late Pre-Pottery Neolithic C (PPNC) village dated to 9120 to 8500 BP. Fifteen other inundated settlements date to the more recent late 8th millennium BP and are associated with the late Pottery Neolithic (PN) Wadi Rabah culture, while another site dates to the slightly earlier PN Lodian culture. All PN sites are located 1–200m offshore at depths of 0–5m below MSL...

In 2012 and 2015, following winter storms, a long, linear boulder-built feature situated at a depth of 3m on the seaward (western) side of the inundated Tel Hreiz settlement was partially exposed. In this article, we demonstrate that the now submerged village was directly associated with this feature, the remains of which we interpret as a seawall. It was deliberately built by the Neolithic villagers and was intended to protect the settlement from waves and marine erosion following post-glacial sea-level rise... The numerous unique features relating to the construction of the Tel Hreiz seawall, plus its orientation, size, shape and seaward location relative to the settlement and adjacent to the paleo shoreline, demonstrate that it was unlikely to have been built for another purpose... The seawall may have worked for a period, however, ultimately it proved futile and the village was eventually abandoned. The Tel Hreiz seawall represents the earliest example of a coastal defence of this type known to date...

It has been suggested, that the substantial stone walls found at the Pre-Pottery Neolithic sites of Jericho (Palestinian Authority) and in Wadi Abu Tulayha and Wadi Ruweishid ash-Sharqi (Jafr Basin, south-east Jordan), were constructed for water management (a barrier for flood water and barrage walls, respectively). These predate the Tel Hreiz seawall; they were built for different purposes and used different construction methods. These examples do however, attest to the abilities of Southern Levantine Neolithic communities in planning, constructing and maintaining installations to control water, as do the excavated and built water wells discovered in several of the submerged Neolithic sites...

The prehistoric submerged villages off the Carmel Coast of Israel were not the only settlements recently found. Since the previous article in *Plos One*, more prehistoric submerged sites came to light, this time from the opposite side of the Atlantic. A recent article in the *USA Today*, dated October 14, 2020, with the title "An Atlantis might wait beneath the Great Lakes. And a group of nonscientists might have the proof," reported of a stone circle along with linear stone arrangements, recently found at the bottom of the lake at the Straits of Mackinac by a team of Native American tribal citizens. If these formations are man-made, it is estimated that they were placed there when the strait's area was last above water—near the end of the last Ice Age, about 10,000 years ago.

It is worth mentioning that the Great Lakes during this time did not exist as we know them today. As the glaciers shifted and retreated, between 9,000 and 11,000 years ago, the water levels in Lake Michigan and Lake Huron were 300 feet lower. This meant that thousands of square miles of fertile land near the water were exposed and available for hunting and new settlements.

Is it possible that the stone circle spotted at the Straits of Mackinac be a hunting structure, as some theorize, or another territorial marker of a prehistoric settlement formed by the same culture who established Atlit Yam on the other side of the World? We must not ignore that genetic migrations indicate that once haplogroup X arrived in the New World, it established itself around Newfoundland and several northeastern states, from Maine to Virginia, and westward around the region of the Great Lakes. Finding signs of prehistoric settlements, stone circles, or territorial markers of concentric rings in this region, including at the bottom of the Great Lakes, would not be a surprise since that was dryland and prime real estate during that period.

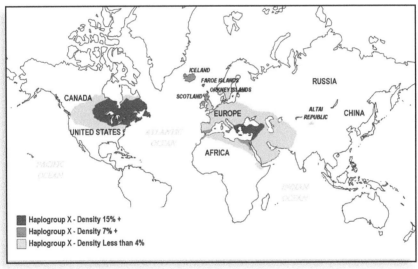

The highest concentration of haplogroup X away from the eastern Mediterranean (the place of origin for haplogroup X) is found around Newfoundland and the Great Lakes of North America and not in Alaska or the west coast where experts claim haplogroup X entered America.

Since haplogroup X's migration to the New World was a real event, evidence of those who brought it will eventually be found, analyzed, and verified. As in the case of a couple of ancient stone circles already found by private landowners in Massachusetts and Virginia, but their significance most likely went unrecognized, let us hope that archaeologists who come across such finds in the future will be more open-minded and not allow taboos or past beliefs to hold back the evidence or to affect their judgment. Considering that many people choose to adhere only to the history they already know, most will never contemplate the prospect that a culture of Middle Easterners can be behind any prehistoric monument found in North America.

Even though the presence of haplogroup X proves that an eastern Mediterranean group reached the New World during our prehistory, such thought would be considered heresy for many. So until an archaeologist brave enough proves otherwise, until then, most "experts" will arrive at the same typical conclusion that all prehistoric sites and stone circles are Paleo-American and were either used for ritual purposes or star observation. Are they, however? Are Native American tribes known to have been obsessed with star observation 10,000 years ago? And what about the fact that a stone circle found in Heath, Massachusetts, resembles other prehistoric stone circles scattered all over England? Is that by sheer coincidence?

While, of course, we have details for every stone circle in England, in the case of the "Burnt Hill Stone Circle" in Massachusetts, no one knows where the twenty-one boulders came from, how the stones were carried on-site (some are enormous), who constructed it, when was it created, or what was its purpose. Researchers first hypothesized that a nineteenth-century farmer erected the rocks as property markers, but as the site appeared to be several hundred years older, that theory was quickly discarded. Some theorized that the hilltop where the megalithic stone circle is located might have been used as an early observatory, but since no one could adequately support this hypothesis, it was soon abandoned too. Others speculated that Native American tribes might have erected the site, but even that remains uncertain. In other words, no one knows how old this site is, who erected it, or what its purpose was.

Another "mysterious" paleolithic site near Bluemont, Virginia, which features a monument of concentric rings of stone, some weighing more than a ton, may resemble the site of Rujm el-Hiri, at Golan Heights. To obtain a professional opinion, this particular property owner reached out to a retired archaeologist who ultimately concluded that the site must have been a Paleo-Indian ritual site. It is worth mentioning that dating analysis found that the monument dates back to 10,470 BC. Knowing this, was the expert accurate in his assessment, or did he allowed himself to arrive at that conclusion since, in his mind, there was no other logical explanation? Were Paleo-Indians known to have been erecting stone circles 12,500 years ago? Not really. Why would they do that, anyway? Such a task would have contradicted their way of life. We know that Paleo-Americans lived in small groups of twenty to sixty individuals and were known to move from place to place as preferred resources were depleted and new supplies were sought. These small family groups were on the move every few days, and they were known to be traveling up to 200 miles per year. In other words, to assume that Paleo-Indians had the time to build stone circles while always on the move would be inconceivable.

The "Burnt Hill Stone Circle," Heath, Massachusetts. (The site is located on private property and is not open to visitors.)

If not Paleo-Indians, though, who else could have erected these stone circles in North America so long ago? Is it possible that those behind haplogroup X (the ones Plato called Atlanteans) are those responsible for these circular structures, or could the Clovis people, another "slightly different Paleo-Indian group," as anthropologists labeled them, have anything to do with that tradition? If so, who were the Clovis, and how do they fit into the big picture?

Archaeologists today will say that the Clovis was a prehistoric Paleo-American culture, primarily known for its distinct stone tools and projectiles. They were also known to behave differently than other Paleo-Americans. They did not rely exclusively on megafauna for subsistence, and they employed a mixed hunting strategy that included smaller game, aquatic animals, and a variety of flora.

Aside from these obvious characteristics, though, experts still are debating who these people were, where they came from 11,500 years ago, and why they vanished three to four centuries later. Although some anthropologists suggested that the Clovis could have ultimately migrated to South America, South America's lack of Clovis artifacts does not support such an assumption.

While other experts in the past also suggested that the Clovis could be the ancestors of most indigenous peoples in the Americas, others quickly point that Paleo-Americans are known to have inhabited North America long before the Clovis people appeared.

It is worth mentioning that once Clovis technology was found in the Americas, researchers also looked for traces of it in Siberia and other places where anthropologists believed the first Americans originated. No traces of Clovis technology in these places were ever found, however. These findings, or better yet, the lack of evidence to support the notion that Clovis migrated to America via the Bering Strait, led most mainstream experts to conclude that Clovis technology must be an American invention. These are the very same people, of course, who insist on protecting the status quo and keep on clinching on the original Bering Strait hypothesis even though recent evidence points to not only one but possibly two transatlantic migrations during our prehistory. As they did in the past, they continue to ignore that the original Solutrean hypothesis, which proposed a migration to America via the Atlantic, was primarily based on the fact that there were distinct similarities between the European Solutrean and the American Clovis lithic technologies.

Should anthropologists, perhaps, under a different migrating scenario, should have further considered the Solutrean hypothesis? As we all know today, the suggestion was primarily dismissed since mainstream academia in the 1970s did not believe that seafaring through the Atlantic was possible at the end of the last Ice Age. Consequently, they elected to go with the Bering Strait hypothesis.

Regrettably, the scientific community not only disregarded Plato's testimony that "the Atlantic was navigable at the time," but they grossly underestimated that a prehistoric civilization could have crossed the Atlantic 11,500 years ago. Even later, during the 1980s, when DNA allowed scientists to follow various haplogroup migrations around the world, they still did not see the clues laid out in front of them. They did not see the traces haplogroup X left behind, like bread crumbs, on every island stop from Europe to North America. Even then, even with all the scientific evidence present, most anthropologists still ignored the obvious and chose to continue to hold on to the Bering Strait hypothesis. Unfortunately for them, though, recent DNA studies once again validate Plato's claim that the migration took place over the Atlantic and via island hopping.

So is there a relationship between the European Solutrean and the American Clovis stone tools? Of course, there is. First and foremost, when analyzing artifacts of the two side by side, they both look identical. Also, considering that the Solutrean culture and technology has been around for several millennia, unlike the American Clovis, which appeared and disappeared 400 years later, clearly points toward the possibility that the Solutrean technology was briefly introduced to the Americas by a small group of migrants who ultimately, over a period of four centuries, assimilated themselves into other local groups.

Taking all these under consideration, knowing the arrival of haplogroup X in North America 11,500 years ago coincided with Clovis's appearance, and when the Atlanteans, according to Plato, came to the New World, is it possible to accept that there is a relationship between these three groups? Of course, there is. All clues point that the Clovis, those Plato referred to as Atlanteans, and those who brought haplogroup X to North America, all three appear to be the same people.

They came to North America about 11,500 years ago, and along with their genes, they brought with them their stone technology and other trades. Clovis points were made for four more centuries afterward and then vanished. So did the culture that created them. If they did not migrate to South America, as some suggested, where did they disappear to? What happened to them?

As these migrants had split themselves into separate groups and settled into different ecological zones, ultimately, they all integrated into their particular environment. And while for a moment it seems that these people came and left in a blink of an eye, their contribution to the New World may be more significant than we realize. Since agriculture in North America started during the ninth millennium BC, and soon after these Middle Easterners appeared, it is conceivable to accept that these early Neolithic farmers could have actually introduced farming skills to local populations and thus help ignite agriculture in the Americas.

What about the prehistoric structures and the stone circles found in North America, however? Is it possible that some of these and particularly those dating between 10,000 BC and 3,000 BC may belong to the same group of Neolithic people? Of course, it is possible. Until additional analysis takes place, though, it will be impossible to know.

The same goes for the find at the Straits of Mackinac. Until further investigation exposes more evidence about the site and the stone circle at the bottom of the lake is further analyzed, we can only speculate who constructed it.

In conclusion, plenty of evidence and clues today establish that the 11,000-year-old Mediterranean civilization Plato said was capable of reaching North America via island hopping is no longer a far-fetched hypothesis. Also, the fact that genetic tests and other evidence help us further identify these people and trace their whereabouts should turn Plato's declaration on Atlantis into a testament that could help answer many of our history's unanswered questions, or "unexplained" events, not to mention "mysterious" artifacts.

One such artifact that puzzled archaeologists and historians for more than a century was the Phaistos Disc. Luigi Pernier discovered the 6-inch-diameter disc in 1908, and it was named after the location where it was found, the Palace of Phaistos on the island of Crete. Although its age cannot yet be conclusively verified, some archaeologists estimate that it could be roughly 4,000 years old. Is it possible that it could be an older artifact? It is certainly a possibility.

The Phaistos Disc, a disc of fired clay, was found in the Minoan Palace of Phaistos, thus its name. The disc is about 15 centimeters (6 inches) in diameter and is covered on both sides with a spiral of stamped symbols.

A Minoan Linear A script used from 1,800 to 1,450 BC

If the disc—as some archaeologists speculate—was created during the Minoan period, why do the symbols on it not match anything else from that period? Furthermore, why a disc with strange characters that were meaningless to its caretakers was carefully stored under Phaistos's palace and, out of all places, in the main cell of an underground temple depository? These basement-type cells were accessible only from above, and they were found to be sealed with a thin layer of plaster. Ironically enough, inside the same cell, and only inches away from the disc, archaeologists uncovered another tablet that had inscribed the language commonly used at the time.

Could the disc be a "souvenir" perhaps from the Minoans' endeavors to other exotic lands, like the New World, for instance? Or is it possible that the Phaistos disc was safeguarded because it belonged to a proto-Minoan civilization and was an ancient artifact from the Minoans' own past?

If so, especially since recent studies proved that the Minoans arose from the same proto-Minoan culture already living on the super-island for 10,000 years, then the symbols on the disc could very well be a proto-Minoan language, one that belongs to the same civilization Plato referred to as Atlantis.

FROM THE AUTHOR

Before I begin, I must confess that never in a million years did I think writing a book would be something that would interest me at any point in my life. Boy, was I wrong! This is my fourth book since 2011.

My first book, *Cyprus: The Island of Aphrodite* (2011), is a travel guide to the Greek Island of Cyprus.

My second book, *Uchronia: Atlantis Revealed* (2014), touches on several controversial topics, including Plato's Atlantis. In 2017, New York City Big Book Awards voted *Uchronia* as one of their distinguished favorites.

My third book, *It's the Economy, Stupid!* (2017), outlines the economic conditions that currently exist in the United States. With dozens of charts and government data covering a period of 60 years, it shows beyond a reasonable doubt that Americans are worse off today than at any other time since 1968. In 2018, the book won two Gold Awards. The first gold was from Independent Press Awards, and the second from the New York City Big Book Awards.

Although my last two books turned out to be award winners, I must say that I do not categorize myself as an expert on the topics I choose to write. Instead, I view myself as a generalist, someone whose knowledge (based on substantial research) can be applied over various subjects, like the economy for instance, and someone who's not afraid to think outside the box.

As a serial entrepreneur, I hold opinions about economics, finance, and public policy. Those who know me know that I love traveling, and I find amusing the occasional mystery that can stimulate one's imagination. I am a professional business owner (in the past 30 years, my company has been renovating large multifamily communities in the southeast United States). I am a real estate investor, an upscale home designer and builder, and an artist. I love working with oil pastels. Although I sold some of my art in the past, I do not see myself as a professional painter either. I am not a historian or archaeologist by profession or an economist; my background certainly does not revolve around the travel industry, yet I choose to write about these subjects despite the fact that some people would question my expertise. I call these my passion projects.

When analyzing the term expert, short of medical experts, who is thought to be an expert these days? According to the dictionary, an expert is someone with extensive knowledge or ability based on research, experience, or occupation in a particular study. In other words, aside from the fact that extensive research meets these criteria, experts are most familiar with a subject matter and can provide some clarity to a complicated question. Are they, though? If experts are meant to shine a light on the issue, why then do we often get conflicting messages and personal opinions from them?

Today, whether watching a news broadcast, a documentary, or an educational program, we are not only showered with the views and perspectives of those who created the show, but we are exposed to some sort of "expert opinion" that either corroborates or, in some cases, contradicts the topic. Particularly, when watching the news nowadays, we are forced to watch a panel of political experts either reiterating live news from their point of view or, worse, see them severely debating or contradicting one another. Most notably, when it comes to politics or the economy, the airwaves get so saturated with crisscrossing "expert opinions," and they often lead to pointless "white noise" and confusion rather than clarity. Why is that, though? Why do specialists often disagree? Is this happening perhaps because even experts are just as vulnerable to cognitive biases as nonexperts? Is it possible that increased specialization on a subject matter often leaves experts failing to appreciate the big picture as often their specialized but narrow perspective cannot adequately integrate into a more complex framework?

For instance, if posing a straightforward question on the economy to five experts, and the result is getting back five distinctly different responses, then this has nothing to do with one's experience or expertise. They are all conveying their personal views on the subject.

The truth is this is happening because not all experts are created equal. According to the dictionary, it appears that experts come in different "flavors" depending on the source of their knowledge. For example, expertise through research or education would be different from expertise gained through experience (not to mention, when all things considered, experts as laymen people do, they observe and understand the world differently from one another).

Nonetheless, let me be clear that by no means am I trying to reject the notion of expertise or suggest that every uninformed person can equally compete in every conversation. Since expertise is a way of which we generally gain knowledge, denouncing it would be like rejecting knowledge itself or, worse, supporting ignorance. On the contrary, all I am trying to convey is that knowledge, in general, is what empowers people to have an educated opinion, while extensive research, in short of expertise, evens the playing field between "experts" and "nonexperts." In a nutshell, anyone who thoroughly researches the US economy and recognizes the mechanics at play can rightfully voice their opinion about it.

The same applies to other fields, like anthropology, archaeology, history, or human evolution. Substantial research allows anyone to have an educated view on these topics as well, especially since decisions in these fields often rely on speculation in the absence of evidence. That explains why getting comparable answers out of experts in these areas, following each discovery, is nearly impossible. Specialists in these professions tend to deliberate and squabble more than in any other line of work, especially when new findings defy a previously established model. The typical way to reach a mutual consensus in these fields, when evidence is limited, is by speculation. For instance, while the age of a recently unearthed structure could easily be analyzed and agreed upon by most archaeologists, if clues are unclear of its function, then its real purpose can remain ambiguous (e.g., Stonehenge, Gobekli Tepe, the Great Sphinx, and others). In these cases, the "loudest" voices or those who can sway the majority tend to decide what becomes the status quo for the rest of us.

Knowing this, are historians, anthropologists, or archaeologists always right in their assessments and ultimate conclusions? Of course not. How many times do we catch ourselves reading an article with a headline, "This discovery will rewrite history as we know it." The truth is as our past continues to unravel with every discovery, we now realize that history is not what we were taught in school decades ago.

This brings me to my second book, *Uchronia*, which means alternative or counterfactual history or history that has not been accepted as real yet by mainstream academia. A neologism created by Charles Renouvier in 1876, it originates from the Greek word *utopia*, replacing *topos* (place) with *chronos* (time), and is typically represented by three types of conjectural work. While one type describes pure fiction stories taking place in entirely imaginary worlds (like the movie *Pandora*, for instance), another concept of uchronia work is based on established history and represents hypothetical realities. This kind of work, for example, considers what would have happened in history if something else had a chance to happen, like Hitler winning World War II. The third type of uchronia contemplates the prospect that a specific event occurred during our history, but this noteworthy event went unrecognized or got misunderstood by the intellectual community. This kind of uchronia work sets a path to explore our missed or misinterpreted past. Such an event was the Trojan War, which for centuries we failed to recognize as a real incident until the ancient city of Troy was ultimately found.

In contrast, if myths or certain hypothetical events can become real over time, what is real history then? When analyzing the term, history seems to be the formal recognition and, ultimately, the written account of particular past events that involve human affairs. How do we arrive at our conclusions, though, for past events to become formally accepted? And is it possible for history to exist without the early speculation that is usually associated with uchronia? The answer is certainly no. If anything, it seems that uchronia works not only help ignite the essential curiosity and conversation vital before any discovery, but speculations often associated with conjectural history frequently set the ground for history to evolve. Without speculation, "mythical" places like the lost city of Ubar (Iram of the Pillars) in the Arabian Peninsula, or the city of Troy in northwestern Turkey, could have never been discovered, and historical events such as the Trojan War could have never been proven real. Time and time again, and more often than we realize, uchronia turns out to be real history.

With this in mind, I thought a chapter with the title "Atlantis Revealed" would be most appropriate in a book called *Uchronia*. Despite the book's rave reviews, though, the truth is over the years, several friends, fans, and foes suggested that Atlantis Revealed, for its weight as a topic, should have been a stand-alone project. So here we are!

This book, with the title *Atlantis: The Find of a Lifetime,* is not just an extension or a more in-depth analysis of the original work published in *Uchronia* but an opportunity to illustrate how several recent discoveries since 2014 validate many conclusions and predictions noted in the earlier study.

Likewise, since many social media followers of the book kept asking for more details behind the scenes, I also felt compelled to reveal more information about the process and clues that led to this find.

Before getting ahead of oneself, though, I must acknowledge that around 2010 when I first started to work on *Uchronia*, a book offering explanations on some of the most contentious mysteries of our time, including that of Atlantis, in truth, I had no idea where to begin on Plato's account. Other than what I have learned in school (where regularly we had to translate Plato and Socrates from ancient Greek to modern Greek before analyzing their scripts, something that helped me tremendously in this case), my information on Atlantis was somewhat limited. Over the years, I've seen a few documentaries and read a few editorials in magazines or newspapers about the subject. Incidentally, I never had the urge to read another author's book since most books on Atlantis nowadays are written by fringe authors, who, over the years, turned Plato's original account of an ancient advanced civilization into a utopian or dystopian fiction.

Before I began my research on *Uchronia*, if anyone asked back then whether I thought there is more to Atlantis's story than meets the eye, my answer would always be most likely. The truth is with every passing decade, an increasing amount of evidence proves that many ancient myths were not myths at all. Just in the case of Troy or the Palace of Knossos, in their storytelling, ancient Greeks are known to introduce real places or events they often wrap in fantastic details and superstition. Atlantis could very well be one of these places.

Out of all available theories on the subject, at the time, I thought the Santorini hypothesis appeared to be the most plausible although I knew very well that by accepting the Santorini setting of 1,600 BC, which had discarded Plato's given chronology along with many elements of the island's physical description, was as if I was acknowledging that Plato's story was just a cautionary tale he created while using the Minoan civilization as a backdrop. Unquestionably, that would have been the case with all other available theories on

Atlantis since none of them ever matched Plato's given description or chronology, not even close!

So from the very beginning, I knew well that for a chapter with the title "Atlantis Revealed" to be convincing, I had to locate a tangible site that in every way matched Plato's physical description. All the physical characteristics, including the given chronology, had to fit perfectly, or this find would have been just another self-proclaimed discovery that would amount to nothing more than speculation.

To successfully decode Plato's puzzle, several English adaptations of Plato's account had to be dissected and thoroughly examined to ensure that they were properly translated. Also, to ensure that the original meaning was not lost during translation, the English versions were compared to the Greek format, which has a different syntactic structure.

Right away, it became evident that all English translations slightly vary from one another. Words, phrases, and sometimes sentences vary from translation to translation. Most importantly, though, I realized that all English translators translated the original Greek document word by word, ignoring that the Greek syntactic structure is very different from the English language we often choose to translate it to. In other words, when a story from ancient Greek is translated to English, as explained in the book, the translated sentences most always require proper repositioning within the paragraph for an English reader to make better sense of it. Not knowing where the emphasis goes in a Greek ancient text (especially before the translation takes place) can cause a great deal of confusion, as often, and depending on where the emphasis goes, two separate meanings can emerge out of the same paragraph. When it comes to ancient Greek, sometimes even a single comma can cause a short sentence to have two meanings. Such an example is a famous quote from the Oracle of Delphi. *"Go, return not die in war"* can have two opposite meanings, depending on where a missing comma is supposed to be—before or after the word *not*.

In short, when Plato's text is correctly understood before a translation takes place, it becomes clear that in regard to Atlantis, Plato was referring to an island within the Mediterranean and not one in the Atlantic Ocean, as many automatically assume when they first read Plato's story in any of the available English versions.

Still, finding a submerged prehistoric island that perfectly matched Plato's description within the Mediterranean was not an easy task. In fact, from time to time, I remember thinking that if all else failed, Santorini could always be used as a contingency although deep down, I knew that the setting of Santorini alone was not what Plato was talking about. While clearly the Minoan aspect in the story matches, the given chronology of 9,600 BC and the primary island of Atlantis are missing from the Santorini setting of 1,600 BC. Failing to match Plato's physical description and chronology was the very reason many skeptics in the past dismissed Santorini as Plato's Atlantis and remained convinced that the story was just a myth.

Indeed, a genuine find requires the chronology and all the elements of the physical description to be present and in the right order. For instance, if Plato said the northern portion of the primary island was covered in mountains that reached the shores, then, by all means, the north part of the lost island had to be entirely covered in mountains that extended to the sea. And if there was an oblong valley just to the south of this mountainous region, once again, this valley had to be oblong (not square or circular), and it had to be just south of the mountainous region, not to the east or west of it, and so on and so forth.

Understanding all this, knowing the task at hand, I remember thinking that the given chronology, which so many researchers tend to ignore when beginning to work on Plato's account, had to be the key to solve this puzzle. A perfect match without the chronology obviously would not be possible; hence, from the very beginning, I acknowledged that the chronology was as crucial as the Powerball number was to a lottery ticket. No jackpot is probable without it.

That decision led me to the next logical conclusion that if such a place exists, it must be under 400 feet of water (since several ocean-ographic studies point that the Mediterranean was about 400 feet lower 11,000 years ago).

So unlike many other researchers who usually begin searching for Atlantis by chasing the details of the story, I decided to ignore the story details for a moment and focus on finding a submerged pre-historic island beneath 400 feet of water. I thought if such a place exists, and I was lucky to find it, I would worry about the details afterward.

So I concentrated my focus on the Mediterranean. Still, finding a prehistoric island under 400 feet of water was not easy until one morning, as I was enjoying a cup of coffee while searching for clues on Google Earth, I came across my lucky break. Somewhere among the Cyclades Islands in the middle of the sea, I noticed the words *Cyclades Plateau*. This caught my curiosity, so I moved the mouse cursor over the general area, somewhere north of the island of Paros, and I noticed that the elevation there was minus 400 feet. Since I was looking for an island under 400 feet of water, I thought that was a good sign, and I moved my cursor to another location slightly to the right. The second location registered minus 392 feet. I moved the cursor again at a third location, which showed the land there was about the same depth. I kept on moving my mouse cursor to several more places until I finally realized this was a gigantic underwater plateau that once upon a time connected several of the Cyclades Islands.

This, undoubtedly, was a promising find although I still had no idea what the entire island looked like or whether it would match Plato's description. All excited, I went straight to Google looking for images of the Cyclades Plateau or the Cyclades Islands during prehistory. I had no luck finding anything though.

It is worth mentioning that, in 2012, when I first tried to find more about the Cyclades Plateau and what the region around the Cyclades Islands looked like ten millennia ago, there were no available images on Google (at least none that I could find). After a couple of hours searching without any luck, I did the next best thing to satisfy my curiosity. With Google Earth's aid, I started using my mouse cursor as a metal detector, and by moving it back and forth and left to right, I would place a pin (a marker) every time the depth registered at minus 400 feet. Several hours later, after I connected all the dots, I was able to identify the perimeter of the prehistoric super-island of the Cyclades Plateau. Only then, only after all the dots were connected, I realized that the partially submerged island, once above water, perfectly matched Plato's given chronology and physical description. Of course, finding Atlantis did not end with the detection and identification of the lost island. That part was only half the work. It took several more weeks to explore the find and understand how Plato's story details compared to the prehistoric submerged island and how those details further corresponded to known historical events.

Today, since *Uchronia* came out, accompanied by a myriad of press releases and images of the prehistoric island I proposed, if anyone goes to Google and looks for the "Cyclades Plateau," you will find dozens of pictures of the prehistoric island (mostly images I created for the book or for marketing purposes) along with others that popped up afterward, primarily by bloggers either approving or contesting the authenticity of my find. Either way, as it seems, *Uchronia* is behind this now popular image.

In regard to a couple of blogger criticisms during 2013, as soon as the book's website went up, I never minded the hard-nosed critique in those because their analysis was entirely based on the book's website (it was as if they were criticizing a book by its cover). More specifically, in the fall of 2013, and while the book was still being prepped for publication, a blogger who visited my website and saw my proposed image posted that, in 2010, geologist K. Gaki-Papanastasiou, in a chapter of the edited volume *Coastal and Marine*

Geospatial Technologies, also had speculated that it is possible that the famous ancient Atlantis, if real, was one of the flourishing city states on the large Cycladic island that was drowned following the rapid sea-level rise between 18,000 and 7,000 years ago.

Not only did I not get upset with this particular "attack," but I was flattered by this revelation so much that I delayed the book's publication long enough so this information can be included in the final version of the book. Indeed, thanks to this blogger, this information is mentioned not only in *Uchronia* but also in this book as well.

My only disappointment, as I remember telling my good friend and business attorney, who read and "blessed" the original manuscript of *Uchronia* before its publication, was finding out that my own image of Atlantis, the one I created with the aid of Google Earth, was only 99.5% and not 100% accurate. And while I truly contemplated correcting the image for a brief moment, in the end, and strictly for sentimental reasons, I decided to keep my original creation since it was nearly identical to the scientific version.

The fact that an academic before me raised the possibility that Plato's Atlantis could have been "a city flourishing on the large Cycladic island" did not bother me because this was a vague assumption on their part that, if anything, further validated my own research. As I pointed out earlier, although finding and identifying the site was challenging enough, this was only half the work. The other half was analyzing, understanding, and explaining how Plato's story corresponded to real history.

Another incident that transpired after the book's publication and is worth mentioning is that during April in 2015, the producers of a well-known series on the History channel reached out to me to "find out whether I would be interested in interviewing for their upcoming season discussing the topic of Atlantis?" After a brief email communication, I called them after the Greek Easter weekend that year, and we talked for a while. I could tell almost immediately that they were a little disappointed to hear me saying that unlike other chapters in *Uchronia,* which touch on the topic of UFOs, the first chapter of the book "Atlantis Revealed" is based entirely on Plato's Atlantis and has nothing to do with extraterrestrials or UFOs. My discovery, I said, being a perfect match to Plato's Atlantis, simply proves once and for all that Atlantis was a real place. Unfortunately, this is not what the show's producers wanted to hear, so I never got to work with them during the following season. My suggestion to create another separate series that is based on mythical places turning real did not appeal to them either.

I thought to mention this incident because another well-known blogger, and self-proclaimed expert on Atlantis, who ironically could not tell the fact that *Uchronia* touches on several controversial topics and not just on Atlantis, he accused me of that very thing. He scolded my discovery because (according to him) I "wasted half of my book on Atlantis talking about UFOs and Ets" and went on to discredit my find with typical jabbers. Evidently, for someone who stresses a scientific method for approaching Atlantis's topic, he seemed oblivious that ridicule is not part of the scientific method. Of course, the most "laughable" part out of that encounter was not the blogger's oddball personality but, in the middle of an abrasive tirade, was seeing him not forget to toss an overbearing sales pitch on his own upcoming book on Atlantis.

Before concluding on what transpired "behind the scenes," though I wanted to use this opportunity to clear another common misconception surrounding Atlantis. It has to do with the mistaken belief that "orichalcum" was a special metal alloy used solely by the Atlanteans.

Recently, it was reported by several news organizations that archaeologists had recovered thirty-nine ingots of orichalcum from a 2,600-year-old shipwreck found ten feet underwater off the coast of Sicily, near the town of Gela. Some called it the "legendary metal," while others referred to it as the "mystical ore" of Atlantis.

While, of course, every news organization capitalized on the particular story by repeating the same misconceptions on Atlantis, none bothered to properly research and correctly report that there is nothing special, mystical, or legendary about orichalcum. Although most reporters at the time automatically connected the ancient freight to Atlantis, they ignored the fact that the particular shipment of orichalcum found off the coast of Sicily most likely could have originated from the Greek island of Cyprus in the eastern Mediterranean. Historically, since the fourth millennium BC, Cyprus has produced every copper variation known to man, including orichalcum, essentially a mixture of copper and zinc with small nickel and iron traces.

During the Bronze Age and especially before the seventh century BC, records show that the word *orichalcum*, which originates from the Greek name *oreichalkos* (a word of two compounding nouns that literally means "mountain copper"), was what the early Greeks called copper (all variations of it). Before the fifth century BC, as the Greeks ruled the eastern Mediterranean, orichalcum, a term that may have also originated in Cyprus, was essentially a common product used not only by the Greeks but by those who traded with them as well.

Historically, the word *orichalcum* began to fade and nearly disappeared from the Greek and Mediterranean vocabulary after the Romans became the region's new masters. Several Greek names, including *oreichalkos* (*orichalcum*), were replaced with their Latin counterparts. Eventually, even the ancient Greeks modified the original name, and *oreichalkos* was ultimately shortened to *chalkos*, which is still in use today by the mainland Greeks.

During the Roman period, Cyprus (*Kypros* in Greek) continued to be the number one copper source for the entire Mediterranean. So much copper was extracted from Cyprus during the Roman era; the Romans originally named the ore after the island itself "*aes-cyprium*" (meaning metal of Cyprus). This phrase ultimately replaced the Greek word *orichalcum* among everyone who used it all around the Mediterranean. Over time, the *aes-cyprium* changed to "*cuprum*" (copper in Latin), and this is where the chemical symbol for copper (Cu) comes from. In modern days, cuprum ultimately changed to "copper," the English version of the Latin name.

Interestingly though, while still many scholars and researchers are debating the origins and composition of orichalcum, most people are not aware that today, more than three thousand years later, the Greek population of Cyprus still call their locally produced copper *oreichalkos* (or *orichalcum*, if you prefer).

While shifting gears for a moment, I wanted to close by sharing a bit of information, a sort of an obstacle I encountered while translating Plato's account. As I pointed out earlier, a genuine discovery requires that all physical elements are present and arranged in the right order, including the given chronology. Indeed, when comparing Atlantis to the super island of the Cyclades Plateau, the prehistoric submerged island unmistakably looked just as Plato depicted.

The northern portion of this island was covered in mountains that reached the shores. There was an oblong valley just south of the mountainous region. Further south of the oblong valley stood another valley two-thirds the size of the oblong valley. Fifty stadia (6 miles or 9 kilometers) away from what was the primary island, and just as Plato mentioned, there was a circular island, an island-within-an-island setting (a sea volcano with a collapsed flooded center). Ships could enter the flooded center of this island via a single opening on the island's outer cliffs and could reach the inner island, which measured 0.57 miles or 0.92 kilometers in diameter. In addition to all other matching elements, flora and fauna on the prehistoric island were also as Plato described. When above water, the island of the "Cyclades Plateau" was heavily forested, while several species of wild animals wandered the land, including elephants.

From the very beginning, everything about this find turned out to be a perfect match. Everything but one thing, a detail that had to be further examined before it was put to rest. This detail had to do with the oblong valley's correct size when considering Plato's measuring methodology. In other words, although the oblong valley on the submerged island at 555 square kilometers perfectly matched Plato's description, it matched as in 555 square kilometers and not as in 555 kilometers long. The fact that Plato used *stadia* to convey the size of the oblong valley (a unit technically referring to length) raised particular concerns and demanded an explanation, whether the measuring unit of *stadia* could be used to denote both length and surface as well.

For example, some of the measuring units used by the ancient Greeks to measure length were the following: *pous* = 1 foot, *haploun bēma* = single step, *diploun bēma* = double step, *orgyia* = 6 feet, *plethron* = 100 feet, *stadion (stadium)* = 600 feet, *diaulos* = 2 stadia, *schoinos* = 40 stadia, *stage* = 160 stadia.

For surface measurements, some of the measuring units the ancient Greeks used to measure an area were the following: *pous* = 1 square foot, *hexapodēs* = 36 square feet, *akaina* = 100 square feet, *aroura* = 2,500 square feet, *plethron* = 10,000 square feet.

Seeing this, right away, it becomes evident that the measuring unit *pous (1 sf)* and the unit *plethron (10,000 sf)* was what commonly they used for measuring both lengths and surfaces, and not *stadia* (stadiums). Is it possible, though, that there was an exception to the rule during Plato's time? Is it possible that during storytelling, an ancient storyteller could use another informal way of conveying measurement? A measuring unit, perhaps, that even a plain audience could more easily relate to?

Today, for instance, while we also are using feet or acres when trying to convey the size of a surface, not surprisingly, we also use city blocks, football stadiums, or stadiums for that matter to describe measurements. For example, today, it is acceptable to say, "Nearly 38,000 solar panels are spread across the land the size of several football fields" (*NPR*). Or say, "Pilgrims will camp out under the stars in an area the size of 48 football fields and hundreds of priests are on hand to listen" (*Telegraph*). Of course, we also use football fields for measuring length too. We also say, "Nearly three football fields long and more than 14 stories high, Iowa is one of the biggest warships ever built (*Los Angeles Times*).

Why is this happening, though? Why do we use nonscientific measuring methods to convey a surface, and is there a significance in that? Is it because a football field is only slightly larger than an acre (1.32 acres), or is it because a football field (or a stadium, if you will) is something that the average person can naturally associate with? The truth is since most people have a good idea of how big a stadium is, we are using football fields to convey the size of a particular piece of land so even the most uninformed person can easily correlate and measure up to. After all, just like square miles or acres, city blocks or stadiums equally can convey land surface.

Knowing this, is it possible to assume that the ancient Greeks could have also slightly twisted the rules and off the record, especially during storytelling, occasionally used stadia (stadiums) to convey surface as well? If by using stadia, Plato meant to quote 555 kilometers in length, a fair question to ask is, Why he chose stadia *(1 stadia = 600 feet)* instead of *stages,* a more appropriate unit to use when measuring a long distance *(a stage measures 2.92 kilometers each)*? As if we measured a room today, we found it to be 20 feet by 50 feet, but for some strange reason, we quoted the dimensions in inches instead of feet or measured a particular topography and found it to be 20 miles wide by 30 miles long but decided to cite it in yards or meters instead of miles or kilometers. Recognizing this and seeing how commonly we use stadiums today to convey land surface, is it possible to accept that this habit may be a collective custom we carried with us over the millennia?

In conclusion, the fact is, for the very first time, there is a real find on Atlantis that meets all the criteria given by Plato. The physical characteristics, one by one, are all present, and all are found to be in the right order, not just on the primary island of Atlantis but also on the circular island-within-an-island setting 9 kilometers away from the primary island. Flora and fauna are there, as well as the volcanic geology. Plato's given chronology also is a match. What are the chances of all that being coincidental? And yet all these would not be enough if a "perfectly matching island" was found to be uninhabited during that period. The fact that an advanced Neolithic civilization occupied the submerged super-island before the Minoans, one that scientists now agree that the Minoans arose from, this further proves that in regard to Atlantis, we may have struck "the lottery's five winning numbers."

Once considering the statistical significance of this find, in regard to whether Plato could have used stadia in this particular storytelling to illustrate the surface of the oblong valley, instead of its length, I am leaving that final detail up to you to decide whether that could be plausible or not.

ABOUT PLATO

Aristocles (428–347 BC), better known to us as Plato, is a nickname that means broad or someone thick set. The ancient writer Diogenes Laertius (third century BC) describes how Aristocles acquired his famous nickname:

> Plato learned gymnastic exercises under the wrestler Ariston of Argos. And it was by him that he had the name of Plato given to him instead of his original name, on account of his robust figure, as he had previously been called Aristocles, after the name of his grandfather, as Alexander informs us in his Successions. But some say that he derived this name from the breadth of his eloquence, or else because he was very wide (platys) across the forehead, as Neanthes affirms. (*Lives and Opinions*, Book III.V)

The child who would grow up to be known as Plato was born either in Athens or the nearby island of Aegina from Athenian parents who lived in Aegina for a while.

Plato's father was Ariston, known as the "inventor of letters" for bringing and introducing the Phoenician alphabet to Greece, and his mother was Perictione, a descendant from the family of the

Athenian politician and lawmaker Solon (c.640–560 BCE). Plato had two brothers, Adeimantus and Glaucon, and one sister, Petone.

Being from an aristocratic family, he was provided with the best education available at the time. He was also taught gymnastics, martial arts by the wrestler Ariston of Athens, music, and mathematics by Metallus of Agrigentum and Draco, son of Damon, the Sophist. He also learned to paint and draw and was introduced to philosophy by Cratylus the Heraclitan (student of Heraclitus, sixth century BCE) and friend of Socrates.

When he was 20 years old, the young Aristocles heard Socrates for the first time teaching at the Agora (market) of Athens, and that, it is said, impressed him so much that it changed young Aristocles forever. He realized that Socrates's teaching was a more noble pursuit than the arts he was engaged in at the time. Therefore, he abandoned all his previous goals, and he became a student of Socrates. For the next 9 years, he remained Socrates's student until 399 BC, when the Athenians executed Socrates on the capital charge of impiety.

After Socrates's death, Plato, as with many other Socrates students, moved away from Athens to avoid a similar fate as his teacher. He moved to Megara, Italy, for a while and then traveled to Egypt. After Egypt, he spent some time in Syracuse, Sicily, before ultimately returning to Athens. In Athens, he founded his academy, which taught geometry, the Socratic method determining the truth, and the philosophical-metaphysical understanding of the nature of reality as expressed in Plato's famous "Allegory of the Cave" from book VII of his *Republic*. At some point after his return, he also began writing his dialogues on truth, good, and beauty, which would establish his reputation and help significantly shape Western thought.

Plato wrote thirty-five dialogues and thirteen letters before he died, emphasizing the immortality of the soul and the realm of objective truth, which had to be acknowledged to live well. Plato's *Republic* and *Laws* consider the ideal state as well as, allegorically, the proper ordering of one's soul.

Plato's most famous dialogue is *Republic*. Professor Forrest E. Baird writes,

> There are few books in Western civilization that have had the impact of Plato's *Republic*—aside from the Bible, perhaps none.

This is not only due to the concepts Plato relates in the *Republic* but also to how he constructs the dialogue to engage a reader in the characters' conversations and arguments. The narrative form Plato manipulates in books I–X of *Republic* takes a reader through the organization of an ideal, just society allegorically the perfect state of an individual soul.

In regard to Atlantis, the only primary sources of that story are Plato's *Timaeus* and *Critias* dialogues. All there is to know about Atlantis and its legendary civilization is contained in these two dialogues. In these, Plato claims he was quoting Solon, who had visited Egypt between 590 and 580 BC and learned of Atlantis from an Egyptian priest.

Plato introduced Atlantis in *Timaeus* at 360 BC.

ATLANTIS
ACCORDING TO PLATO

Atlantis (in Greek, Ἀτλαντὶς νῆσος, which means "island of Atlas") is a legendary island first mentioned in Plato's dialogues of *Timaeus* and *Critias*, written about 360 BC. According to Plato, Atlantis was a naval power that approximately 9,600 BC had conquered many parts of Europe and Africa.

Although, as previously mentioned, Plato's translated story on Atlantis varies from translation to translation, for practical purposes, the following translated excerpts on Atlantis (unless otherwise noted) are by R. G. Bury.

> Listen then, Socrates, to a tale which, though passing strange, is yet wholly true.

> Of the citizens, then, who lived 9,000 years ago.

> Now first of all we must recall the fact that 9000 is the sum of years since the war occurred, as is recorded, between the dwellers beyond the pillars of Heracles and all those that dwelt within them.

For it is related in our records how once upon a time your State stayed the course of a mighty host, which, starting from a distant point in the Atlantic Ocean, was insolently advancing to attack the whole of Europe, and Asia to boot. For the ocean there was at that time navigable; for in front of the mouth which you Greeks call, as you say, "the pillars of Heracles," there lay an island which was larger than Libya and Asia together; and it was possible for the travelers of that time to cross from it to the other islands, and from the islands to the whole of the continent over against them which encompasses that veritable ocean. For all that we have here, lying within the mouth of which we speak, is evidently a haven having a narrow entrance; but that yonder is a real ocean, and the land surrounding it may most rightly be called, in the fullest and truest sense, a continent." (*Timaeus* 24e–25a, R. G. Bury translation [Loeb Classical Library])

Now in this island of Atlantis there existed a confederation of kings, of great and marvelous power, which held sway over all the island, and over many other islands also and parts of the continent; and, moreover, of the lands here within the Straits they ruled over Libya as far as Egypt, and over Europe as far as Tuscany.

An island comprising mostly mountains in the northern portions and along the shore, and encompassing a great plain of an oblong shape in the south "extending in one direction three thousand stadia [about 555 km; 345 mi], but across the center inland it was two thousand stadia [about 370 km; 230 mi]." Fifty stadia [9 km; 6

mi] from the coast was a mountain that was low on all sides...broke it off all round about...the central island itself was five stades in diameter [about 0.92 km; 0.57 mi]. (*Critias* 113, 116a)

But at a later time there occurred portentous earthquakes and floods, and one grievous day and night befell them, when the whole body of your warriors was swallowed up by the earth, and the island of Atlantis in like manner was swallowed up by the sea and vanished; wherefore also the ocean at that spot has now become impassable and unsearchable, being blocked up by the shoal mud which the island created as it settled down. (*Timaeus* 25c–d)

It was stated that this city of ours was in command of the one side and fought through the whole of the war, and in command of the other side were the kings of the island of Atlantis, which we said was an island larger than Libya and Asia once upon a time, but now lies sunk by earthquakes and has created a barrier of impassable mud which prevents those who are sailing out from here to the ocean beyond from proceeding further.

Poseidon...to make the hill impregnable he broke it off all round about; and he made circular belts of sea and land enclosing one another alternately, some greater, some smaller, two being of land and three of sea, which he carved as it were out of the midst of the island; and these belts were at even distances on all sides, so as to be impassable for man; for at that time neither ships nor sailing were yet in existence.

And they covered with brass, as though with a plaster, all the circumference of the wall which surrounded the outermost circle; and that of the inner one they coated with tin; and that which encompassed the acropolis itself with orichalcum which sparkled like fire.

Metals, to begin with, both the hard kind and the fusible kind, which are extracted by mining, and also that kind which is now known only by name but was more than a name then, there being mines of it in many parts of the island,—I mean "orichalcum" which was the most precious of the metals then known, except gold.

Now as a result of natural forces, together with the labors of many kings which extended over many ages, the condition of the plain was this. It was originally a quadrangle, rectilinear for the most part, and elongated; and what it lacked of this shape they made right by means of a trench dug round about it. Now, as regards the depth of this trench and its breadth and length, it seems incredible that it should be so large as the account states, considering that it was made by hand, and in addition to all the other operations, but none-theless we must report what we heard: It was dug out to the depth of a plethron and to a uniform breadth of a stade, and since it was dug round the whole plain its consequent length was 10,000 stades. It received the streams which came down from the mountains and after circling round the plain, and coming towards the city on this side and on that, it discharged them thereabouts into the sea. And on the inland side of the city chan-nels were cut in straight lines, of about 100 feet

in width, across the plain, and these discharged
themselves into the trench on the seaward side,
the distance between each being 100 stades. It
was in this way that they conveyed to the city the
timber from the mountains and transported also
on boats the seasons' products, by cutting trans-
verse passages from one channel to the next and
also to the city.

Now the country was inhabited in those days by
various classes of citizens: there were artisans,
and there were husbandmen, and there was a
warrior class originally set apart by divine men;
these dwelt by themselves, and had all things
suitable for nature and education; neither had
any of them anything of their own, but they
regarded all things as common property; nor
did they require to receive of the other citizens
anything more than their necessary food. And
they practiced all the pursuits which we yesterday described as those of our imaginary guard-
ians. Also, about the country the Egyptian priests
said what is only probable but also true, that the
boundaries were fixed by the isthmus, and that
in the other direction they extended as far as the
heights Cithaeron and Parnes; the boundary line
came down towards the plain, having the district
of Oropus on the right, and the river Asopus on
the left, as the limit towards the sea. The land
was the best in the world, and for this reason was
able in those days to support a vast army, raised
from the surrounding people. And a great proof
of this fertility is, that the part that still remains
may compare with any in the world for the variety and excellence of its fruits and the suitable-
ness of its pastures to every sort of animal; and

besides beauty the land had also plenty. How am I to prove this? And of what remnant of the land then in existence may this be truly said? I would have to observe the present aspect of the country, which is only promontory extending far into the sea away from the rest of the continent, and the surrounding basin of the sea is everywhere deep in the neighborhood of the shore. Many great deluges have taken place during the nine thousand years, for that is the number of years which have lapsed since the time of which I am speaking; and in all the ages and changes of things, there has never been any settlement of the earth flowing down from the mountains as in other places, which is worth speaking off; it has always been carried round in a circle and disappeared in the depths below. "The consequence is, that in comparison of what then was, there are remaining in small islets only the bones of the wasted body, as they may be called, all the richer and softer parts of the soil having fallen away, and the mere skeleton of the country being left. But in former days, and in the primitive state of the country, what are now mountains were regarded as hills; and the plains are they are now termed, of Phelleus were full of rich earth, and there was abundance of wood in the mountains. Of this last the traces still remain, for there are some of the mountains which now only afford sustenance to bees, whereas not long ago there were still remaining roofs cut from the trees growing there, which were of a size sufficient to cover the largest houses; and there were many other high trees, bearing fruit, and abundance of food for cattle." (*The Dialogues of Plato: Republic/ Timaeus. Critias*-Plato, Benjamin Jowett)

BIBLIOGRAPHY

"464 BC Sparta earthquake." https://en.wikipedia.org/wiki/464_BC_Sparta_earthquake.

"464 B.C. The Helot Revolt of Sparta Greece." https://aurorak12.org/gateway/academics/Social%20Studies%20Dept.%20Pages/documents/FINALTheForceofChangeinSpartaHelotRevolt.pdf.

"A Submerged 7000-Year-Old Village and Seawall Demonstrate Earliest Known Coastal Defence Against Sea-Level Rise." *Plos One*. https://journals.plos.org/plosone/article?id=10.1371/journal.pone.0222560.

Novo Scriptorium. "A 7,000 Years Old Submerged Coastal Defence Attempt (Sea-Wall) Found at Tel Hreiz, Israel." https://novo-scriptorium.com/2020/04/02/a-7000-submerged-coastal-defence-attempt-sea-wall-found-at-tel-hreiz-israel/.

"Aeolipile." https://en.wikipedia.org/wiki/Aeolipile.

"Ancient DNA Analysis Reveals Minoan and Mycenaean Origins." *Phys Org Journal*. https://phys.org/news/2017-08-civilizations-greece-revealing-stories-science.html.

Britannica. "Ain Ghazal." https://www.britannica.com/place/Ain-Ghazal.

"Ain Ghazal." https://en.wikipedia.org/wiki/%27Ain_Ghazal.

"Ali Kosh." https://www.britannica.com/place/Ali-Kosh.

"Ali Kosh." https://en.wikipedia.org/wiki/Ali_Kosh.

"An Atlantis Might Wait Beneath the Great Lakes. And a Group of Nonscientists Might Have the Proof." *Detroit Free Press*.

https://www.usatoday.com/story/news/nation/2020/10/14/straits-mackinac-ice-age-culture-native-american-tribes-great-lakes/3649437001/?fbclid=IwAR0YLMyphECpFMtHhWnzC1jBU7UWaUQweyReJB5J_KQbTMnZ-5zzRSgzv38.

"Archeologists Find Evidence of Rapidly Rising Sea Levels in Israel 7,000 Years Ago." JewishPress.com. https://www.jewishpress.com/news/on-campus/archeologists-find-evidence-of-rapidly-rising-sea-levels-in-israel-7000-years-ago/2019/12/19/.

Science Daily. "Archaeologist 'Strikes Gold' with Finds of Ancient Nazca Iron Ore Mine in Peru." 2008. http://www.sciencedaily.com/releases/2008/01/080129125405.htm.

"The Ancestry and Affiliations of Kennewick Man." https://www.nature.com/articles/nature14625.

"Atlantis." http://en.wikipedia.org/wiki/Atlantis.

"Atlit Yam." https://en.wikipedia.org/wiki/Atlit_Yam.

"Bat Creek Inscription." http://en.wikipedia.org/wiki/Bat_Creek_Inscricption.

American Petrographic Services, Inc. "Bat Creek Stone Investigation." http://www.ampetrographic.com/files/BatCreekStone.pdf.

"The Builders of World's Oldest Known Temple Had a Surprising Understanding of Geometry." https://www.sciencealert.com/world-s-oldest-known-temple-reveals-mysterious-knowledge-of-geometry-scientists-say.

"Black Sea Deluge Hypothesis." http://en.wikipedia.org/wiki/black_sea_deluge_hypothesis.

"Burnt Hill Stone Circle, Heath, Massachusetts. A Mysterious Collection of Stones Stand Outside a Small New England Town." *Atlas Obscura.* https://www.atlasobscura.com/places/burnt-hill-stone-circle.

Turkish Archaeological News. "Çayönü Archaeological Site and Hilar Caves Face Oblivion." https://turkisharchaeonews.net/news/%C3%A7ay%C3%B6n%C3%BC-archaeological-site-and-hilar-caves-face-oblivion.

Khan Academy. "Çatalhöyük." https://www.khanacademy.org/humanities/prehistoric-art/neolithicart/neolithic-sites/a/atalhyk.

DNA Consultants. "Cherokee Unlike Other Indians." https://dna-consultants.com/cherokee-unlike-other-indians/.

"The Clovis Point and the Discovery of America's First Culture." *Smithsonian*. https://www.smithsonianmag.com/history/the-clovis-point-and-the-discovery-of-americas-first-culture-3825828/.

"Clovis Culture." https://en.wikipedia.org/wiki/Clovis_culture.

"Couple Discovers Stone Circles on Property." *The Roanoke Times*. https://roanoke.com/news/virginia/couple-discovers-stone-circles-on-property/article_1a74e748-d8b5-11e3-9cfa-0017a43b2370.html.

"Copper Mining in Michigan." http://en.wikipedia.org/wiki/copper_mining_in_michigan.Curry, Andrew.

"The Greeks Really Do Have Near-Mythical Origins, Ancient DNA Reveals. *Science*. https://www.sciencemag.org/news/2017/08/greeks-really-do-have-near-mythical-origins-ancient-dna-reveals.

"Gobekli Tepe: The World's First Temple." November, 2008. http://www.smithsonianmag.com/history-archaeology/gobekli-tepe.html.

"Cup and Ring Mark." https://en.wikipedia.org/wiki/Cup_and_ring_mark.

"Dating Do-Over for Anzick-1, Famous First Americans Burial." https://www.discovermagazine.com/planet-earth/dating-do-over-for-anzick-1-famous-first-americans-burial.

"DNA Analysis Unearths Origins of Minoans, the First Major European Civilization." https://www.washington.edu/news/2013/05/14/dna-analysis-unearths-origins-of-minoans-the-first-major-european-civilization/.

"mtDNA Haplogroup X: An Ancient Link Between Europe/Western Asia and North America?" *PMC Journal*. https://www.ncbi.nlm.nih.gov/pmc/articles/PMC1377656/.

Doughton, Sandi. "Kennewick Man Yields More Secrets." http://seattletimes.com/html/localnews/2002825565_kennewick24m.html.

Doumenge, Francois. Presentation on "The Mediterranean Crisis." United Nations University Headquarters. July 15, 1996.

"Early Cycladic Art and Culture." https://www.metmuseum.org/toah/hd/ecyc/hd_ecyc.htm.

"Evidence of Cosmic Impact at Abu Hureyra, Syria at the Younger Dryas Onset (~12.8 ka): High-temperature melting at >2200°C." *Scientific Reports Journal.* https://www.nature.com/articles/s41598-020-60867-w.

Archaeology. "First Farmers." https://archive.archaeology.org/0011/abstracts/farmers.html.

"Five Baffling Discoveries That Prove History Books Are Wrong." *Huff Post,* June 12, 2013.

"Flood Myth." http://en.wikipedia.org/wiki/flood_myth.

Gaki-Papanastasiou, K. "Geoarchaeology of the Cyclades During the Holocene; Does the Underwater Morphology Provide Clues for the Lost Atlantis?" In *Coastal and Marine Geospatial Technologies,* edited by Dr. D. R. Green, 302.

"Ganj Dareh." https://en.wikipedia.org/wiki/Ganj_Dareh.

"Gobekli Tepe: Geometry Guided Construction of 11,500-Year-Old Megalithic Complex." http://www.scinews.com/archaeology/gobekli-tepe-geometry-08424.html.

"Gobekli Tepe: The World's First Temple?" *Smithsonian.* https://www.smithsonianmag.com/history/gobekli-tepe-the-worlds-first-temple-83613665/.

Genet, Am J. Hum. "DNA Haplogroup X: An Ancient Link Between Europe, Western Asia, and North America." *The American Journal of Human Genetics* (December 1998). http://www.cell.com/AJHG/retrieve/pii/50002929707616292.

"Great Flood." *New World Encyclopedia.*

"Hall of Records." http://en.wikipedia.org/wiki/hall_of_records.

Penn Museum. "Hallan Çemi." https://www.penn.museum/sites/expedition/intricacies-of-hallan-cemi/.

"Hal Saflieni Hypogeum." https://en.wikipedia.org/wiki/%C4%A6al_Saflieni_Hypogeum.

"Isle Royale." http://en.wikipedia.org/wiki/Isle_Royale.

Jowett, Benjamin. *The Dialogues of Plato: Republic, Timaeus, Critias.*

"Kennewick Man." http://www.en.wikipedia.org/wiki/Kennewick_man.

Britannica. "Jericho." https://www.britannica.com/place/Jericho-West-Bank.

"Jericho." https://en.wikipedia.org/wiki/Jericho.

"Jarmo." https://en.wikipedia.org/wiki/Jarmo.

"Judging, Expertise, and the Rule of Law." *Washington University Law Review.* https://core.ac.uk/download/pdf/233179345.pdf.

"Kennewick Man Is Native American." https://dnaexplained. com/2015/06/18/kennewick-man-is-native-american/.

"Khirokitia." http://en.wikipedia.org/wiki/khirokitia.

"Kukulkan." http://en.wikipedia.org/wiki/kukulkan.

"Large-Scale Cereal Processing Before Domestication During the Tenth Millennium cal BC in Northern Syria." https:// citeseerx.ist.psu.edu/viewdoc/download?doi=10.1.1. 722.2736&rep=rep1&type=pdf.

Licking, Ellen. "Don't Blame the Horse: Earthquakes Toppled Ancient Cities, Stanford Geophysicist Says." (November 11, 1997). http://news.stanford.edu/pr97/971112nur.html.

"Landslide at Mt. Etna Generated a Large Tsunami in the Mediterranean Sea Nearly 8000 Years Ago." *Science News.* https:// www.sciencedaily.com/releases/2006/11/061128083754.htm.

"List of Stone Circles." https://en.wikipedia.org/wiki/List_of_stone _circles#Brazil.

"Long Meg and Her Daughters." https://en.wikipedia.org/wiki/ Long_Meg_and_Her_Daughters.

"Massive Crater under Greenland's Ice Points to Climate-Altering Impact in the Time of Humans." *Science.* https://www.science-mag.org/news/2018/11/massive-crater-under-greenland-s-ice-points-climate-altering-impact-time-humans.

"The Mystery of the Black Sea Floods Solved." *Journal of Earth Science & Climatic Change.* https://www.omicsonline. org/open-access/the-mystery-of-the-black-sea-floods-solved-2157-7617-1000489-104841.html.

"Map of Greece at Current and at Late Glacial." https://www. researchgate.net/figure/Map-of-Greece-at-current-and-at-Late-Glacial-100m-sea-levels-courtesy-of-A_fig1_265865249.

"Maya Civilization." http://en.wikipedia.org/wiki/maya_civilization.

"Minoan Colonies in America?" http://greeceandworld.blogspot. com/2013/08/minoan-colonies-in-america.html.

"Nevalı Çori." https://en.wikipedia.org/wiki/Neval%C4%B1_ %C3%87ori.

UNESCO. "Neolithic Site of Çatalhöyük." https://whc.unesco.org/ en/list/1405/.

"On Crete, New Evidence of Very Ancient Mariners." https://www. nytimes.com/2010/02/16/science/16archeo.html.

"One Engineer's Crazy Plan to Drain the Mediterranean." https://www.mentalfloss.com/article/558376/ one-engineers-crazy-plan-drain-mediterranean.

PaleoAmerica: A Journal of Early Human Migration and Dispersal. https:// www.tandfonline.com/doi/pdf/10.1179/2055556315Z.00000 000040?needAccess=true.

"Paleo-Indians." https://en.wikipedia.org/wiki/Paleo-Indians.

"Persian Gulf Once Dry, Green, and Inhabited by Humans: Implications." Biot #422: May 15.

"Plato's TIMAEUS: Atlantis Against Athens." https://www.ellopos. net/elpenor/physis/plato-timaeus/atlantis-athens.asp?pg=4.

"Pliny, Natural History." http://www.attalus.org/translate/pliny_ hn36a.html.

"Pliny the Elder." http://en.wikipedia.org/wiki/pliny_the_elder.

"Pre-Columbian Trans-oceanic Contact." http://en.wikipedia.org/ wiki/pre-columbian_trans-oceanic_contact.

"Primitive Humans Conquered Sea, Surprising Finds Suggest." *National Geographic.* https://www.nationalgeographic.com/ news/2010/2/100217-crete-primitive-humans-mariners-sea-farers-mediterranean-sea/.

"Quetzalcoatl." http://en.wikipedia.org/wiki/Quetzalcoatl.

"Republic, Timaeus, Critias." https://books.google.com/ books?id=h8o9AAAAYAAJ&pg=PA597&lpg=PA597&d-q=The+consequence+is,+that+in+comparison+of+wha

t+then+was,+there+are+remaining+in+small+islets+on-
ly+the+bones+of+the+wasted+body,+as+they+may+be+-
called,+all+the+richer+and+softer+parts+of+the+soil+hav-
ing+fallen+away&source=bl&ots=pjMlOKoVXb&sig=AC-
fU3U1rJY6VI4p8VbxG_poFnt7vlfmlnw&hl=en&sa=X-
&ved=2ahUKEwjV5LW3wPrrAhVHU98KHS-
4kADMQ6AEwBnoECAcQAQ#v=onepage&q=The%20
consequence%20is%2C%20that%20in%20compari-
son%20of%20what%20then%20was%2C%20there%20
are%20remaining%20in%20small%20islets%20only%20
the%20bones%20of%20the%20wasted%20body%2C%20
as%20they%20may%20be%20called%2C%20all%20the%20
richer%20and%20softer%20parts%20of%20the%20soil%20
having%20fallen%20away&f=false.

"Rising Seas Swallowed Countless Archaeological Sites. Scientists Want Them Back." *Discover*. https://www.discovermagazine.com/planet-earth/rising-seas-swallowed-countless-archaeological-sites-scientists-want-them-back.

"Rio Artifacts May Indicate Roman Visit." *The New York Times*. https://www.nytimes.com/1982/10/10/world/rio-artifacts-may-indicate-roman-visit.html.

Armstrong Economics. "Roman Coins Wash Up on Beach in Florida. https://www.armstrongeconomics.com/history/ancient-history/roman-coins-wash-up-on-beach-in-florida/.

Ryan, W. B. and W. C. Pitman. "Black Sea Deluge Theory." *Chemistry Daily*. http://www.chemistrydaily.com/chemisty/black_sea_deluge_theory.

Bureau of Land Management. "Staking a Claim." https://www.blm.gov/programs/energy-and-minerals/mining-and-minerals/locatable-minerals/mining-claims/staking-a-claim.

"Shanidar Cave." https://en.wikipedia.org/wiki/Shanidar_Cave.

"Sphinx's New Riddle—Is It Older Than Experts Say?: Archeology: Geologists Cite Study of Weathering Patterns. But Egyptologists Say Findings Can't Be Right. *Los Angeles Times*. https://www.latimes.com/archives/la-xpm-1991-10-23-mn-183-story.html.

"Stonehenge: DNA Reveals Origin of Builders." BBC. https://www.bbc.com/news/science-environment-47938188.

"Stone Circles Found on Virginia Property." *The Winchester Star.* https://www.newsleader.com/story/news/local/2014/05/11/stone-circles-found-on-virginia-property/8974715/.

"The Strange Origin of Scotland's Stone Circles." BBC. http://www.bbc.com/earth/story/20161012-the-strange-origin-of-scotlands-stone-circles.

"Scientists Find Evidence of 'Ghost Population' of Ancient Humans." https://www.theguardian.com/science/2020/feb/12/scientists-find-evidence-of-ghost-population-of-ancient-humans.

Symmes, Patrick. "History in the Remaking." *Newsweek.* http://www.questia.com/library/1g1-219477534/history-in-the-remaking.

"Tell Aswad." https://en.wikipedia.org/wiki/Tell_Aswad.

"Theory of Phoenician Discovery of the Americas." http://en.wikipedia.org/wiki/Theory_of_Phoenician_Discovery_of_the_Americas.

"Unknown Civilizations: Tell Mureybet." TDJ World News. http://thedailyjournalist.com/the-historian/unknown-civilizations-tell-mureybet/.

Science Alert. "Vast DNA Analysis of Hundreds of Vikings Reveals They Weren't Who We Thought." https://www.sciencealert.com/giant-dna-analysis-of-hundreds-of-ancient-vikings-reveals-they-weren-t-who-we-thought.

Living DNA. "What Are Haplogroups? Living DNA explain." https://livingdna.com/blog/haplogroups-explained.

"X mtDNA Haplogroup." https://www.familytreedna.com/groups/x/about/background.

NOTES

1. "Antikythera Mechanism," Wikipedia, the Free Encyclopedia, http://en.wikipedia.org/wiki/antikythera_mechanism.

2. "Atlantis," Wikipedia, the Free Encyclopedia, http://en.wikipedia.org/wiki/Atlantis.

3. "Rio Artifacts May Indicate Roman Visit," *New York Times*, https://www.nytimes.com/1982/10/10/world/rio-artifacts-may-indicate-roman-visit.html.

4. "Roman Coins Wash Up on Beach in Florida," Armstrong Economics, https://www.armstrongeconomics.com/history/ancient-history/roman-coins-wash-up-on-beach-in-florida/.

5. "Massive Impact Crater Beneath Greenland Could Explain Ice Age Climate Swing," *Discover* magazine, https://www.discovermagazine.com/environment/massive-impact-crater-beneath-greenland-could-explain-ice-age-climate-swing.

6. "Rising Seas Swallowed Countless Archaeological Sites. Scientists Want Them Back," *Discover* magazine, https://www.discovermagazine.com/planet-earth/rising-seas-swallowed-countless-archaeological-sites-scientists-want-them-back.

7. "DNA Analysis Unearths Origins of Minoans, the First Major European Civilization," University of Washington, https://www.washington.edu/news/2013/05/14/dna-analysis-unearths-origins-of-minoans-the-first-major-european-civilization/.

8. "mtDNA Haplogroup X: An Ancient Link Between Europe/Western Asia and North America?, US National Library of Medicine National Institutes of Health, https://www.ncbi.nlm.nih.gov/pmc/articles/PMC1377656/.

9. "Does Mitochondrial Haplogroup X Indicate Ancient Trans-Atlantic Migration to the Americas? A Critical Re-Evaluation," *PaleoAmerica* journal, https://www.tandfonline.com/doi/full/10.1179/2055556315Z.00000000040.

10. "Primitive Humans Conquered Sea, Surprising Finds Suggest," *National Geographic*, https://www.nationalgeographic.com/news/2010/2/100217-crete-primitive-humans-mariners-seafarers-mediterranean-sea/.

11. James C. Chatters, "Kennewick Man," http://oneyahweh.com/w/archives/201.

12. Charles Gallenkamp, *Maya: The Riddle and Rediscovery of a Lost Civilization* (1987).

13 T. J. O'Brien, *Fair Gods and Feathered Serpents* (1828).

14 John D. Baldwin, "The Phoenician Theory," Wikipedia, the Free Encyclopedia, http://en.Wikipedia.org/wiki/theory_of_phoenician_discovery_of_the_americas.

15 Ian Driscoll and Matthew Kurtz, *Atlantis: Egyptian Genesis*, 60.

16 "Atlantis," Wikipedia, the Free Encyclopedia, http://en.wikipedia.org/wiki/atlantis #cite_ref-7.

17 Ibid.

18 Ibid.

19 "Dialogues of Plato, Volume 2, Plato's Critias," Wikipedia, the Free Encyclopedia, http://en.wikipedia.org/wiki/Ancient_Greek_flood_myths#cite_ref-1.

20 Ibid.

21 Ibid.

22 K. Gaki-Papanastasiou, *Coastal and Marine Geospatial Technologies*, 302.

23 "Pliny The Elder," Loeb Classical Library, https://www.loebclassics.com/view/pliny_elder-natural_history/1938/pb_LCL419.61.xml?readMode=recto.

24 "Stonehenge: DNA Reveals Origin of Builders," BBC News, https://www.bbc.com/news/science-environment-47938188.